CONCILIUM

CONCILIUM
ADVISORY COMMITTEE

REGINA AMMICHT-QUINN	GERMANY
MARÍA PILAR AQUINO	USA
MILE BABIĆ OFM	BOSNIA–HERZEGOVINA
JOSÉ OSCAR BEOZZO	BRAZIL
WIM BEUKEN	BELGIUM
MARIA CLARA BINGEMER	BRAZIL
LEONARDO BOFF	BRAZIL
ERIK BORGMAN OP	HOLLAND
CHRISTOPHE BOUREUX OP	FRANCE
LISA SOWLE CAHILL	USA
JOHN COLEMAN	USA
EAMONN CONWAY	IRELAND
MARY SHAW COPELAND	USA
ENRICO GALAVOTTI	ITALY
DENNIS GIRA	FRANCE
NORBERT GREINACHER	GERMANY
GUSTAVO GUTIÉRREZ OP	PERU
HILLE HAKER	USA
HERMANN HÄRING	GERMANY
LINDA HOGAN	IRELAND
DIEGO IRRARÁZAVAL CSC	CHILE
WERGNER G. JEANROND	SWEDEN
JEAN-PIERRE JOSSUA OP	FRANCE
MAUREEN JUNKER-KENNY	IRELAND
FRANÇIOS KABASELE LUMBALA	DEMOCRATIC REPUBLIC OF CONGO
HANS KARL-JOSEPH KUSCHEL	GERMANY
SOLANGE LEFEBVRE	CANADA
MARY-JOHN MANANZAN	PHILIPPINES
DANIEL MARGEURAT	SWITZERLAND
ALBERTO MELLONI	ITALY
NORBERT METTE	GERMANY
DIETMAR MIETH	GERMANY
JÜRGEN MOLTMANN	GERMANY
PAUL D. MURRAY	UK
SAROJINI NADAR	(SOUTH AFRICA)
TERESA OKURE	NIGERIA
AGBONKHIANMEGHE OROBATOR SJ	KENYA
ALOYSIUS PIERIS SJ	SRI LANKA
SUSAN A. ROSS	USA
GIUSEPPE RUGGIERI	ITALY
LÉONARD SANTEDI KINKUPI	DEMOCRATIC REPUBLIC OF CONGO
SILVIA SCATENA	ITALY
PAUL SCHOTSMANS	BELGIUM
ELISABETH SCHÜSSLER FIORENZA	USA
JOHN SOBRINO SJ	EL SALVADOR
JANET MARTIN SOSKICE	UK
LUIZ CARLOS SUSIN OFM	BRAZIL
ELSA TAMEZ	COSTA RICA
CHRISTOPH THEOBALD SJ	FRANCE
ANDRÉS TORRES QUIERUGA	SPAIN
DAVID TRACEY	USA
ROBERTO TUCCI	ITALY
MARCIANO VIDAL	SPAIN
JÕAO J. VILA-CHÃ SJ	PORTUGAL
MARIE-THERES WACKER	GERMANY
ELAIN M. WAINWRIGHT	NEW ZEALAND
FELIX WILFRED	INDIA
ELLEN VAN WOLDE	HOLLAND
CHRISTOS YANNARÁS	GREECE
JOHANNES ZIZIOULAS	TURKEY

CONCILIUM 2025/1

Nicaea After 1700 Years. Critical Insights into a Living Legacy

Edited by

Luca Ferracci, Stephan van Erp, Susan Abraham

Published in 2025 by SCM Press, 3rd Floor, Invicta House, 110 Golden Lane, London EC1Y 0TG.

SCM Press is an imprint of Hymns Ancient & Modern Ltd (a registered charity) 13A Hellesdon Park Road, Norwich NR6 5DR, UK

Copyright © International Association of Conciliar Theology, Madras (India)

www.concilium.in

English translations copyright © 2025 Hymns Ancient & Modern Ltd.

All rights reserved. No part of this publication may be reproduced, stored in a retrieval system, or transmitted, in any form or by any means, electronic, mechanical, photocopying or otherwise, without the prior written permission of the Board of Directors of Concilium.

ISBN 978-0-334-06675-0

EU GPSR Authorised Representative
LOGOS EUROPE, 9 rue Nicolas Poussin, 17000, LA ROCHELLE, France E-mail: Contact@logoseurope.eu

Concilium is published in March, June, August, October, December

Contents

Editorial	7
The reception of the Nicene-Constantinopolitan Creed beyond the Roman *limes*: the case of the Goths GIACOMO FREDA CIVICO	13
An Apology of the Nicene Orthodoxy for Muslims: Elias of Nisibis' Commentary on the Creed BISHARA EBEID	20
Introducing Trinity and Avoiding Trimurti: The Reception of the Trinitarian Doctrine of the Nicene-Constantinopolitan Creed in Early Modern India PAOLO ARANHA	30
What does Nicaea have to do with Manila?: Theological Gaps and Contextualization in Filipino Christology AUSTIN ORTINERO	40
The liturgical "decanonisation" of the Nicene-constantinopolitan Creed. Inserting the "Apostolic" Creed in the Post-Vatican II Ordo Missae MASSIMILIANO PROIETTI	49
The Nicene-Constantinopolitan Creed in the editions of Communio (1972-1975). A struggle for Catholic identity? GUISEPPE SAMUELE ADORNO	59

Beyond the Filioque Controversy and the Symbols of Faith: 68
The Rise of Pentecostal, Charismatic and Non-Denominational
Christianity
VALENTINA CICILIOT

Contributions from feminist theology to trinitarian theology. 77
Reimagining the notion of "relationality"
SILVIA MARTÍNEZ CANO

On the origins of the ecumenical re-appropriation of the Nicene 88
faith (19th century)
LUCA FERRACCI

"Confessing the One Faith" 98
The contribution of a Faith and Order study to the anniversary
of the Council of Nicaea
JOHANNES OELDEMANN

Theological Forum

Toward an understanding of Ratzinger's assertion of an 111
"inalienable right of Greek thought to a place in Christianity"
FÁINCHE RYAN

Nicaea as Symbol of Faith and Symbol of Tragedy? 119
STEVEN BATTIN

Contributors 130

Editorial

Every Sunday, Christians all over the world recite the Nicene Creed as a confession of faith, but most do not know that the Creed was not conceived to become what it actually has been throughout the eighteen centuries of its history: a cornerstone for all Christian denominations, circulating in the most diverse theological settings, with a wide impact on local cultures and diverse theological, political and philosophical implications. Created for mainly liturgical and catechetical purposes, the Creed has shown a double capacity for adaptation: of a cultural kind, as a bridge towards mission populations, and of a linguistic kind. Translations of the Creed begun as early as in the fourth century (produced in the Armenian, Syriac, and Coptic regions and, later, also in the Arab world) and the expansion of Christianity during the Modern Age has resulted in the production of translations into even more diverse languages, from Slavonic to the idioms spoken in each of the so-called "mission lands".

In 2025, the year in which the Christian churches and the academic world celebrate the 1700th anniversary of the Council of Nicaea, *Concilium* provides with this issue an opportunity to revisit and reflect on old discussions, as well as to propose new approaches and interpretative frameworks. In accordance with an interdisciplinary and transcultural approach, this issue offers thirteen original studies by scholars who each examine an aspect of the legacy of the Creed, trying to demonstrate its profound heritage and cultural adaptability with fresh, sometimes provocative, but always intellectually rich ideas.

The first four essays deal with the issue of the "reception" of the Creed in cultures far from the Greek-Latin cultural context. In some cases, these populations had settled within the borders of what had been the Roman Empire, but without sharing the orthodoxy of Nicaea that was forming and unifying western Christian intellectual culture in late antiquity. This was the situation of the Goths, presented in the essay by **Giacomo Freda**

Editorial

Civico, who, although they rejected the Nicene orthodoxy in favor of a subordinationist creed, adapted its philosophical-theological categories to their own cultural canons to be alternative but equal interlocutors with the Latin world. In other cases, the Symbol has been a means to defend and explain the Christian faith to non-Christians. **Bishara Ebeid** in his essay presents the case study of the *Commentary* on the Nicene Creed composed by Elias the East-Syrian Metropolitan of Nisibis at the beginning of the 11th Century to address the Muslim accusation that Nicaea was the cause of the corruption of the Christian faith, where the Trinitarian doctrine was invented and replaced the authentic monotheistic faith taught by Christ. However, in the case of Elias of Nisibis, the apologetic intent was also related to the attempt to make the Christian understanding of the Trinity more accessible to a Muslim audience, using accepted methods and intelligible language by his opponents. Especially during the Modern Age, when the missionaries were committed to spreading the principles of "true faith" among "pagans", this led to an "accommodationist" approach to local cultures. Obviously, this process of adaptation had its basic principle in the Creed that missionaries translated (usually from the Latin) and shaped according to the language and the worldview of the mission populations. But this has not prevented the surface of global Christianity from being furrowed by deep gaps in the local reception of the Trinitarian faith. This is the emphasis of the essays offered by **Paolo Aranha** and **Austin John Millares Ortinero**. While Aranha analyses how the similarity between the Hindu Trimūrti and the Christian Trinity has been interpreted in different ways by the missionaries and the Church authorities in the early modern India (either a relic or a prefiguration of Christianity, or alternatively a diabolical mockery of it), **Austin John Millares Ortinero** identifies the lack of a Filipino philosophy that can translate the full weight of the *homoousios*, the overemphasis on the humanity of Christ, and the development of a local Christology as three possible reasons of the partial understanding of the Creed in the Philippines' popular religiosity.

In the West, the Creed has always oscillated between two complementary functions: transmitting the faith and preserving its orthodoxy. In the Roman Catholic tradition, there have been times when the second function has prevailed over the first. In 1968, during the celebration at the conclusion of the Year of Faith and amid the tumultuous reception of Vatican II, Paul

Editorial

VI pronounced *The Creed of the People of God*, a solemn profession of faith written by his friend, the philosopher Jacques Maritain. The text of this Credo retraced the one formulated at the council of Nicaea, but with the interpolation of later dogmas like original sin, the real presence of Christ in the Eucharist, the primacy of Peter, the virginity of Mary, the Immaculate Conception, and the Assumption. This new profession of faith was to replace the Oath against Modernism instituted by Pius X in 1910, but the intent remained the same: to reaffirm the continuity of the Roman Catholic doctrine and protect the "faith of the simple" from the spread of a materialistic worldview and the progress of contemporary theology. As **Samuele Adorno** shows, the pope was supported in this mission by the theologians of the journal *Communio*, which devoted several issues between 1972 and 1975 to the Nicene-Constantinopolitan Creed and the problem of de-hellenization of the faith. What was at stake for them was the defense of the patristic *logos* as the expression of the universality of the Christian faith, and it was precisely around the problem of how the church should communicate revelation to modern human beings that the debate between *Concilium* and *Communio* on the legacy of Vatican II has revolved for so long.

This brings us to the other side of the matter, which is the transmission of the faith of the People of God (*traditio fidei*). This is a function that the Nicene-Constantinopolitan Creed has fulfilled through its nature as a "liturgical" creed, given its constant presence in the liturgy of the Mass since the Council of Trent. **Massimiliano Proietti** writes that this "monopoly" of the Nicene Creed over the Catholic Mass ended with the liturgical reform of Vatican II, which rediscovered the Apostles' Creed, which was easier to translate into vernacular languages and more appropriate for the new Mass and the rite of baptism. This process of "de-canonization" of the Nicene Creed also occurred at the linguistic and conceptual level. **Silvia Martínez Cano** writes passionately about how feminist theologies are contributing to re-signify the Trinitarin faith with new languages and metaphors, often bringing new perspectives and an interdisciplinary approach leading to a revival for theology.

It is important to note that not all Christian communions in the West take the Nicene faith as a valid expression of the apostolic teaching. It is often said that the emergence and the spread on a global scale of Pentecostal-like and non-denominational churches have obscured the centrality of the symbols of faith in contemporary Christian identity, given the dogmatism with which these symbols have been clothed in pneumatological discourse. But in some respects, this is an assumption that is only partially true. As **Valentina Ciciliot** asserts, although the symbols of faith were practically unnecessary, when not initially rejected, in the rise of Pentecostal and charismatic Christianity, the contemporary ecumenical dialogue with the other Christian confessions has demanded classical Pentecostals to reopen the debate on the Creed and thus to give it a chance as a statement of the common faith.

Indeed, the approaching anniversary of 2025 seems to have awakened the churches from their torpor (some have called it the "ecumenical winter"), convincing them to resume the ecumenical journey. There are conditions for the 6th World Conference on Faith and Order, which will take place in October 2025 under the motto 'Where Now for Visible Unity?', to produce important results that this issue unfortunately cannot report on. Similarly, we can only hope that the wish of Pope Francis and Patriarch Bartholomew to meet in Nicaea to celebrate the sacrament of Communion together will be realized, as hoped for by the two leaders in 2024. What this issue offers in the meantime are two analyses of the historical and theological roots of the ecumenical significance of the Creed today. **Luca Ferracci** writes about how in the 19th Century the Nicene-Constantinopolitan Symbol was rediscovered as the cornerstone of Christian unity by theologians that historicized and thus relativized doctrinal differences between the churches, allowing them to redescend into the heart of the Christian faith. **Johannes Oeldemann**, recalls a study document published in 1991 by the Faith and Order Commission, which offers an ecumenical explication of the Nicene-Constantinopolitan Creed.

Finally, our two forum essays by **Fáinche Ryan** and **Steven Battin** try to revitalize a conversation that remains as important now as it was in the fourth century: i.e. the relationship between Greek thought and Christian faith, and question whether Aristotelian-Thomistic and colonial categories are suitable for expressing the perennial truth of revealed faith. In the late 20th century the emerging paradigm of "World Christianity" sharply polarized the literature on the Nicene-Constantinopolitan Symbol, especially in the field of theology. In contrast to Joseph Ratzinger's theory about the Nicene Creed as the cornerstone of a process of hellenization of Christianity, which is binding for other cultures (as he explained in his elucidation of the Apostles' Creed, first published in 1968 under the title *Introduction to Christianity*), theologians such as Wolfahrt Pannenberg, Hans Urs von Balthasar and Hans Küng interpreted the Nicene-Constantinopolitan Creed as a dynamic reality bearing universal ecumenical significance for the contextualization of the Christian faith.

Ryan's argument is that, while Ratzinger undoubtedly argues for the authenticity and providential interaction of Christian tradition with Greek thought, his work can be read as nonetheless being in principle open to an exploration of religious pluralism and interreligious dialogue to the extent that Greek thought is understood as the only medium within which intercultural interaction can take place. In congruence with decolonial theorists, instead, Battin argues that Nicaea has a "tragedy side" that reverberates through Christian history, contributing in its own way to colonial modernity's penchant for refusing dialogue with the indigenous Other and denying to the indigenous Other epistemic and spatial autonomy.

The reception of the Nicene-Constantinopolitan Creed beyond the Roman *limes*: the case of the Goths

GIACOMO FREDA CIVICO

The reception of the Nicene-Constantinopolitan Creed among the Goths is a particular case study. Traditional historiography has focussed on how the Germanic peoples were anti-Nicene from the beginning of evangelisation. However, little attention has been paid to the dynamics of conversion, which outline a much more complex and varied panorama, or to the doctrinal trends present in the first centuries, or above all to the circumstances of this apparent total rejection. This article analyses how it was not a unambiguous rejection and how some figures have contstructed an anti-Nicene doctrine thanks to a theological-philosophical and linguistic sensitvity.

The reception of the Nicene-Constantinopolitan Creed beyond the Roman border, among the Goth people, is a matter for particular study. The general opinion is that these people in fact rejected the Nicene-Constantinopolitan Creed, even while some historiographies differ on which doctrinal party was the majority. However, some sources testify to how the start of the evangelisation of this people preceded the years of the Arian controversy.[1]

To fully understand the diversity of Christian trends at the beginning of this evangelisation, it is necessary to analyse the process of Christianisation in its initial phases, i.e. those of the mid-third century CE. In this period of military anarchy, the first Christian groups spread among the Gothic people. Some of these, such as Ulfilas' ancestors, were slaves captured from the cities of Cappadocia during military raids. These subordinate and servile people were able to influence a wider section of the population, on the one hand due to the mass of domestic slaves, and on the other due to the high social mobility that characterised the Goths as a nomadic people, as indicated by the case of Ulfilas himself, of Cappadocian lineage but with a Gothic name (*Wolf* – "little wolf"). Of course, it is likely that the number of Christian slaves was small, but other evangelising forces can be considered. For example, the Gothic army was very permeable: in a moment of great hostility from the imperial institutions, quite a few Christians decided to enlist in the Germanic militias, acquiring both wealth from the loot and an important social position[2]. Marriage policies and limited commercial and civil contacts between the Goths and the Dacian environment also contributed to the process of Christianisation, as evidenced by the presence of imported Christian cultic objects from the third century, and locally produced from the fourth century, indicative of a significant Christian community.[3]

This picture indicates the presence of various Christian communities which were already formed and organised in the years of the Council of Nicaea and the Arian crisis. In fact, the reception of the Nicene-Constantinopolitan Creed took place in an apparent almost total rejection and massive adoption of subordinationism. "Apparent", because various theological tendencies are attested among the Goths, testifying to a certain philosophical-theological sensitivity, often downplayed by traditional historiography. These tendencies are Nicene, Arian, and others, such as the Audian tendencies, which, due to their example of ascetic isolation, perhaps represent the greatest threat to the social order[4]. The Nicene nuclei, amongst other things, persisted even when the majority of the population had adopted subordinationism and when the Goths themselves were in a position of political-military superiority[5]. In the past, the rejection of the Creed has been attributed to a different cultural sensitivity, which would have taken on a demeaning traditional cultic model to reproduce it again within a new religion[6]. However, this factor of "comprehensibility" could only partly explain the reason for its diffusion, but not that of the triumph of Arianism, both because it does not focus attention on evangelising figures, and because it does not take into account a multifacted and varied phenomena in which different churches and Christianity coexisted Furthermore, traditional Gothic beliefs are almost completely unknown, and this criterion is based on a supposed similarity between the Gothic religion and the Germanic religion of the first century testified by Tacitus.

It is appropriate to analyse the evangelisers, key figures belonging to a cultural elite educated in the great cities of the Empire. They, more than the population, had a strong philosophical and theological sensitivity. Much of the credit for the triumph of Arianism goes to these, in particular to the work of Ulfilas. Consecrated bishop by Eusebius of Nicomedia, educated in Constantinople, he was the author of a new alphabet in order to translate the Bible into the Gothic language. This cultural work implies an unparalleled accessibility to the Christian message, differentiating the evangelising mission of its followers from the unsystematic one promoted by other doctrinal currents. Furthermore, Ulfilas' teacher, Bishop Theophilus, as defined in the *laterculus* of Nicaea *Gothiae*, participated in the Council of Nicaea. Almost certainly of anti-Nicene faith, despite subscribing to the Creed, as was usual for the majority of figures opposed to the Creed, he was the head of the major Church of the Goths, as indicated by his participation at Nicaea itself. This importance, combined with the uniformity that a written text was able to give to the Christian message, explains how the reception of the Nicene-Constantinopolitan Creed was carried out in partial rejection.

It should be underlined that the Gothic *societas* viewed in Christianity a socio-cultural character in which it could recognise itself at the level of identity rather than in the intimate sphere. In particular, the literature arising with the new alphabet represented a new cultural heritage in which to recognise oneself in a phase of ethnogenesis, of forty-year migrations and changes. This literature is distinguished by the fact that it deals with purely religious topics: it is an exegetical literature. From it, it is possible to obtain not only an in-depth knowledge of contemporary doctrinal tendencies, but also the methods of constructing the rejection of the Creed of Nicaea and Constantinople. As with the entire Arian crisis, the term that causes problems is ὁμοούσιος. This lexeme had undergone modifications, rejections, and readmissions, which can also be seen in Gothic literature itself, proving the theological-religious sensitivity of this population and how it constructed the rejection of the Creed by taking up the arguments arising from the numerous conciliar discussions which marked the whole of the fourth century.

Some examples can help us to support this statement. A fifth-century exegetical excerpt, the *Skeireins aiwaggeljons þairh Johannen* (Commentary on the Gospel of John), is full of hints about the Arianism of the Germans and how they understood the various shades of the meaning of the term. Preserved in two miscellaneous copies between the end of the fifth and the beginning of the sixth century[7], this text, whose linguistic translation or redaction is still discussed, has a *post quem* date of 449, since it takes up some passages from the Commentary of Cyril of Alexandria. In folio V, in particular, it is explicitly stated that the Son must be given *an honour that is not equal but similar* to that given to the Father; furthermore, at the end of the folio, speaking of the love addressed to the Father, this formula is repeated, which echoes the homea of 357. Here the *hapax legomenon ibnaleiks* is used to mean "equal", a new formula that combines the adjectives *ibna* "equal" and *galeiks* "similar" in the same definition. This adjective could also be expressed with the word *ibna* regarding the meaning; instead, here the construction with the word *galeiks* is preferred. One theory[8] suggests that the three terms are used in correspondence with Greek terms: *ibna* for ἴσος, *galeiks* for ὅμοιος and *ibnaleiks* for ὁμούσιος. However, this theory cannot be proven[9]. If *ibna* and *galeiks* differentiate the two Persons of the Trinity, *ibna* and *ibnaleiks* express the same concept, but with two different shades of meaning, otherwise a specific new formula would not have been used in the text. Since there are no differences between the two adjectives on a semantic level, it is probable that the second word expresses the concept of "similar in everything" or "similar in substance", expressions used by non-Nicene doctrinal parties.

In addition to the nuances of meaning relating to the traditions of similar and equal, in common with Greek, there is also an evident use of attributes aimed at distinguishing the figures of the Trinity, both in the Gothic literary tradition and in the Latin report of the doctrines of Gothic bishops. In the *Skeireins* there is a redundant juxtaposition between the father, *atta* or also called *guþ* "god" and the son, *sunus* or *fraujia* "lord", as well as the juxtaposition between *ainabaura* "only begotten", referring to the son, and *unbauranamma*" "not incarnate" addressed to the father, of greater divinity as he was not generated and indeed not incarnated. The word *ainabaur* plausibly follows either the Latin formula *unigenitus filius* or the Greek μονογενής and is more suitable for identifying the differences of the Trinitarian Persons compared to *sunus ainaha*, thus underlining the detachment from the theology confirmed in Nicaea. There are also other Latin testimonies that indicate not only a high-level theological preparation on the part of the Gothic authors, but also the adoption of the typical subordinationist language. An example of how these figures constructed the rejection of the Creed is contained in ms. *Parisinus* 8907: between the lines of a commentary by Bishop Maximinus on the documents of the Council of Aquileia, there is an examination of Ulfila's faith written by his disciple Auxentius of Durosturum, which ends with a profession of faith by the master himself. This is short, which provoked a discussion about Ulfila's doctrinal affiliation, whether it was Omean, and therefore moderate, or Eunomian, and radical; a text of just a few lines is, on the one hand, easier to understand, but on the other hand more difficult to be countered by potential informers[10]. In his analysis of his master's faith, Auxentius uses numerous attributes addressed to the Father, to underline his greater divinity, fitting into a now traditional anti-Nicene practice. He goes so far as to define the Son as *secundus deus*, suggesting an extreme position toned down in the Ufilian Creed for reasons of brevity.

In conclusion, the reception of the Nicene-Constantinopolitan Creed in the Germanic context, resulted in a general, but not total, rejection. The rejection of the symbol passes through a careful theological construction, with both cultural and linguistic bases. If the criterion of comprehensibility has almost been overcome, the role of evangelising figures, now on a cultural level of equality with the great imperial exegetes, must be reconsidered; but also the sense of identity. In fact, in addition to the philosophical-theological sensitivity that moved the missionary bishops, their other great merit was that of having provided a new cultural heritage for self-recognition. Worship in Germanic societies had a public dimension, functioning as a social aggregator. Sharing a ritual and common beliefs provided the basis for belonging to the ethnic group. In a time of great changes, migrations, and mixing with Greco-Roman culture, Gothic literature, imbued with a subordinationist Christian sense, provided a valid substitute to traditional cults now unsuitable for the new society which had formed. Furthermore, the identity plan also had a fundamental role in the following centuries, which also explains the resistance to the Nicene-Constantinopolitan Creed in Western *kingdoms*. Once settled in the imperial regions, the Goths and the other Germans who followed tended to adopt new cultural canons, taking up the Roman ones and re-adapting them to their own society (cf. the Theodoric *civilitas*). If on the one hand there was a sense of imitation of the Latin world, on the other there was also a desire to stand out, placing themselves as equal interlocutors. Subordinationism, whether homeian or extremist, in this context, satisfied these feelings, as there is a Christianity in common with the Greco-Roman world, but at the same time a notable distinction at the doctrinal level.

Translated by Patricia Kelly

Notes

1 Cfr. Commodian, Carmen apologeticum, 807-822; Sozomen, HE, II 6, 2; Patr. Nicean. nomina, XLII., XLIII., Eusebius, Const. II 53-III 7; Philostorgius, II 5; sources collected in Nico De Mico/ Simonetta Marchitelli/ Simona Rota, Fonti per la cristianizzazione dei Germani (secc. IV-VIII), Rome: Herder, 2007, pp.535-580; cfr. Viola Gheller, "Prima di Ulfila, accanto a Ulfila: missionari (in)volontari tra i Goti", in Emanuele Piazza (eds.), Qui est quiligno pugnat?: Missionari ed evangelizzazione nell'Europa tardantica e medievale (secc. IV-XIII), Verona: Alteritas, 2016, pp. 54-63.
2 Cfr. Rosalba Arcuri, "Forme di dipendenza nelle società barbariche dell'Occidente tardoantico: incidenza economica e strutture sociali", in Jordi Cortadella i Morral/ Oriol Olesti Vila/ César Sierra Martìn (eds.), Lo viejo y lo nuevo en las sociedades antiguas: homenaje a Alberto Pireto, Besançon: Presses Universitaires de Franche-Comté, 2018, 470–482; Walter Pohl, "Introduction", in Walter Pohl/ G. Heydemann (eds.), Strategies of Identification: Ethnicity and Religion in Early Medieval Europe, Turnhout: Brepols publisher, 2013, 1–64; Mario Caravale, Ordinamenti giuridici dell'Europa medievale, Bologna: il Mulino, 1994, 15–25; Herwig Wolfram, Geschichte Der Goten, Munich: C.H. Beck'sche Verlagsbuchhandlung, 1979, translated from German to Italian, Storia dei Goti, Rome: Salerno Editrice, 1985, 164–175.
3 See also: Giorgio Bejor/ Maria Teresa Grassi/ Stefano Maggi/ Fabrizio Slavazzi, Arte e archeologia nelle province romane, Milan: Mondadori, 2011; Chris Thomas, "Claudius and the Army Reforms," Historia: Zeitschrift Für Alte Geschichte 53/4 (2004), 424–452; Peter Heather, The Goths, Oxford: Blackwell Publishing, 1996, 35–39; Stepehn Johnson, Late Roman Fortifications, Tortona: Barnes & Noble Imports, 1982; Eugen Lozovan e Safia Haddad, "Dacia sacra," History of Religions 7/3 (1968), 209–243; George Leonard Cheesman, The Auxilia of the Roman Imperial Army, Oxford: Clarendon Press, 1914.
4 Epiphanius, panar. 70, 14, 5-15, 5, in De Mico/ Marchitelli/ Rota, Fonti per la cristianizzazione dei Germani, 542s. See also Gheller, "Prima di Ulfila", accanto a Ulfila, 51–55.

5 See: Basil, epist. 164; Paulinus of Nola, carm. 12, 197–268; Jerome, epist. 106, 1-2; Girolamo. 107, 2; John Chrysostom, epist. Ad Olymp., 15, 5; John Chrysostom, epist. 207; John Chrysostom, hom. 2, 3; John Chrysostom, hom. 8; Sources in the collection: De Mico/ Marchitelli/ Rota, Fonti per la cristianizzazione dei Germani, 539ss, 564–573.
6 Heinz-Eberhard Giescke, Die Ostgermanen und der Arianismus, Leipzig: Teubner, 1939, 57 ss; Cfr. Bruno Luiselli, Storia culturale dei rapporti tra mondo romano e mondo germanico, Rome: Herder, 1992, the third part of the volume, "L'età romano-barbarica", subdivided into four chapters which anaylse the period from the third to the eighth centuries.
7 Otto fogli manoscritti: Ambrosiana: cod. E 147, 77–80, 111–114, 309–310: Vaticana: cod. lat. 5750, 57–62.
8 Gustav Ernst Dietrich, "Die Bruchstücke der Skeireins," Texte und Untersuchungen zur altgermanischen Religionsgeschichte, 1903, 69.
9 Raffaella Del Pezzo, Skeireins: Commento al Vangelo di Giovanni, Naples: Istituto Universitario Orientale, 1997, 90.
10 Manilo Simonetti, La crisi ariana nel IV secolo, Rome: Institutum Patristicum Augustinianum, 1975, 211–353; Manilo Simonetti, "L'arianesimo di Ulfila", in Manilo Simonetti (ed.), Studi di Cristologia Postnicena, Rome: Institutum Patristicum Augustinianum, 2006, 167–187; Manilo Simonetti, "Arianesimo latino," Studi Medievali 8/2 (1967), 663–667; Tarmo Toom, "Ulfila's Creedal Statement and Its Theology," Journal of Early Christian Studies 29 (2021), 525–552.

An Apology of the Nicene Orthodoxy for Muslims: Elias of Nisibis' *Commentary on the Creed*

BISHARA EBEID

Some medieval Muslim theologians considered Nicaea to be the cause of the corruption of the Christian faith, where the Trinitarian doctrine was invented and replaced the authentic monotheistic faith taught by Christ. The Commentary on the Nicene Creed, composed by Elias the East-Syrian Metropolitan of Nisibis (d. 1049), should be viewed not only as a polemic against non-East Syrian Christians but also as a Christian apology that addresses Muslim accusations against the Trinitarian and Christological dogmas. In this article, I analyze this aspect of Elias' Commentary on the Creed.

1. Introduction

Elias of Nisibis (975-1046) was one of the most significant East-Syrian authors of the 11th century. His extensive writings reveal his profound knowledge in various fields, including medicine, mathematics, philosophy, Arabic and Syriac philology, ethics, Christian theology, and Islamic speculative theology. This article aims to analyze certain elements of the Trinitarian section of his *Commentary on the Creed*, considering the work not only as a polemic against non-East Syrian Christians but also as a Christian apologetic response to Muslim accusations against Christian doctrines.[1]

2. Elias of Nisibis and the Muslim Critique Against the Nicene Creed

Elias was a man of dialogue engaging in debates with scholars from various religions and Christian denominations. Between July 15 and 29, 1027, he met with the Muslim vizier Abū al-Qāsim al-Maġribī (d. 1027), a prominent Šīʿī Muʿtazilī scholar of his time, where they discussed a range of topics. After the vizier's death, Elias wrote and published the *Book of Sessions*, which detailed his discussions with al-Maġribī. This work was methodically divided into seven sessions, organized rationally and thematically.[2]

Among the discussed topics between the two scholars was the Nicene Creed. In the *First Session*, which focuses on Trinitarian Doctrine, the vizier al-Maġribī refers to the Creed twice. In the first instance, he quotes a section of it and then argues that the Creed confirms the belief in three gods:

> He [the vizier] said: 'Don't they [i.e. Christians] profess that God is substance, three hypostases, Father, Son, and Holy Spirit?'. I said: 'Indeed we profess that!'. He said: 'Don't you accept the Creed that was decided and composed by the Three Hundred Eighteen [Fathers]? I answered: 'Indeed we accept it and glorify it!'. He said: 'Then, your doctrine that God is three hypostases—Father Son, and Holy Spirit—is blasphemy and polytheism and the Creed decided by the Three Hundred Eighteen [Fathers] contains that Jesus, who for you is the human taken from the virgin Mary, is Lord, Creator not created'.[3]

It is not surprising to read such an accusation against the Nicene Creed from a Muslim scholar. Among Muslim scholars and theologians, this accusation had become traditional. It is stated that at Nicaea, under the influence of Constantine the Great, the doctrine on the Trinity was invented, contradicting monotheism—the true faith and doctrine of Jesus and his Gospel. According to this accusation, the Trinity is interpreted and understood as Tritheism.[4] Inventing the doctrine on the Trinity also entails developing the teaching on the Son of God and his incarnation, another aspect that Muslims do not accept, even if they recognize Christ as a prophet sent from God.⁵ This was the argument in the second instance where the vizier referred to Nicaea and its Creed in the *First Session*.⁶

One might then wonder how the Metropolitan of Nisibis reacted to these accusations; however, it is not the focus of this article.⁷ Nonetheless, it is evident from the quotation above that Elias does not reject the Creed and its contents but refutes the interpretation given to it by his Muslim interlocutor.

3. The Authority of Nicaea and its Creed in Elias' Theological Writings

In Elias's response to the vizier's critique, one can also observe the great authority the Creed of the Three Hundred and Eighteen Fathers holds for him. This authority is evident in many of his theological writings, like his *Book of the Demonstration of the Correctness of the Faith*, which can be considered a presentation of the identity of the Church of the East from doctrinal, historical, liturgical, and ethical perspectives.

In this book, Elias aims to distinguish his community from other Christian Churches living in the Abbasid Caliphate and beyond. The work is divided into four sections, each containing several chapters arranged according to a specific logic: starting with the doctrine of the Trinity, then proceeding to Christological issues, and finally discussing various Christian virtues and duties related to liturgical and ecclesiological topics pertinent to his Church. Although the work is written primarily as an apology directed at other Christian denominations, mainly Miaphysites and Chalcedonians, the material on the Trinity and other topics was composed, mainly with Jews and Muslims in mind.⁸

Elias in his *Demonstration* dedicates a small paragraph to the Council of Nicaea, mentioning that it was convened during the reign of Emperor Constantine, and asserting that the reason for the council was the heresy of Arius.⁹ Elias does not provide additional information about the council or even its Creed, instead, he focuses on listing the names of the East Syrian bishops who participated in the council, identifying them as among the Three Hundred and Eighteen Conciliar Fathers. This emphasis on the East Syrian participants serves an apologetic function: by highlighting their involvement in composing the Nicene Creed, Elias argues that the Christology of the Miaphysites and Chalcedonians contradicts the Nicene

Creed, whereas the doctrine of the East Syrians does not.[10]

Additionally, in his *Demonstration*, Elias frequently underscores that the faith of the East Syrians aligns with the teachings of the Gospels and the Apostles.[11] Consequently, he presents the doctrine of the Three Hundred and Eighteen Fathers as apostolic, adhering to the teachings of the Gospels. While this agreement is declared indirectly in his *Demonstration*, it is presented more explicitly in his *Commentary on the Creed*. In this work, for each doctrinal article, Elias quotes verses from the Old and New Testaments to demonstrate its correctness and agreement with the Scripture.[12]

4. The *Commentary on the Creed* as an Apology for Muslims

The critiques against the Nicene Creed, addressed to Elias by the Muslim vizier, were likely one of the reasons that led our metropolitan to compose his *Commentary* and even to entitle it as follows: "The *Commentary on the Creed,* which the Three Hundred and Eighteen Fathers, who were chosen by Constantine, the Byzantine Emperor (May God have Mercy on Him!) have agreed on its composition" (vv. 2-3).[13] By choosing this title, Elias asserts that although the Creed was composed by the participants convened by Emperor Constantine, this does not mean that its doctrine was invented. This is, in fact, the aim of the *Commentary*, which also functions as an apology in response to the accusations of Muslims against the Christian faith, as well as those of the Chalcedonians and Miaphysites against the East Syrians.

Elias' work belongs to the genre of *Commentaries* on the Nicene Creed, which has been used in the patristic tradition since the fourth century. The primary purpose of such commentaries was catechetical, explaining the tenets of the Christian faith to those who wished to become baptized. However, in the Arab-Christian heritage, this genre expanded its audience. Arab-Christian authors used their commentaries to explain to the members of their churches both 1) the Christian faith, in defense against the accusations of Muslims and Jews, and 2) the proper Christological dogma, in response to other Christian confessions. It is clear, then, that the genre evolved from being primarily catechetical and baptismal to entering the literary genre of Christian apologetics.[14] Elias' *Commentary* is indeed a clear example of this dual apologetic function.

The structure of the *Commentary* is as follows: citing a section of the Creed in Syriac, providing an Arabic translation of it, and then offering an interpretation of this section. At the end of the nineteen sections, there is a final prayer. It is noteworthy that the author does not cite the Creed according to its original Nicene version but instead uses the Nicene-Constantinopolitan Creed, which was likely accepted by the Church of the East in 544. A careful reading of the Syriac text reveals that Elias faithfully follows the liturgical version of the Creed. Nevertheless, it is also probable that he considers the version found in the *Synodicon Orientale*, the collection of the acts of the synods of his Church. Elias is faithful in his translation from Syriac. However, one finds in some sections slight variations which demonstrates that when he modifies or elaborates on his Arabic translation of the Syriac text, he does so for theological reasons.[15]

All this leads to the assertion that: 1) At his time, there was not yet an official Arabic text of the Creed adopted by the Church of the East; 2) The Syriac text had to be translated into Arabic and also interpreted; 3) The translation required some modification and elaboration, so that 4) it could be understood. 5) The translation and its interpretation could function as a manual for East Syrians for catechetical, apologetic, and polemic purposes.

In his *Commentary*, and mainly in its Christological material, Elias polemicizes against the doctrine of Miaphysites and Chalcedonians (called respectively Jacobites and Melkites), mentioning them by name (vv. 69, 135). Here, however, I aim to highlight how this *Commentary* also functions as an apology directed at Muslims, even if they are not mentioned by name. To realize this objective, and in addition to my previous arguments concerning the *Commentary*'s title and the author's use of the Bible—which should be considered reactions against the Muslim critiques of Nicaea—I will examine the Trinitarian material in the *Commentary*.

5. The *Commentary*'s Trinitarian Material and the Muslim Accusations of Tritheism

In many of his apologetic writings addressed to Muslims, and sometimes to Jews, composed in defense of the Trinitarian doctrine, Elias employs philosophical argumentation based on triads, syllogisms, natural analogies,

Biblical proofs, and the Islamic doctrine of the divine attributes. His approach is aimed at convincing his opponents that: 1) Believing in the Trinity is not tritheism; 2) Christians are also monotheists.[16] This approach is evident in the interpretation he gives to the Trinitarian sections of the Nicene Creed.

For Elias, Christians believe in one God: the Father, the Son, and the Holy Spirit. The oneness of God pertains to His substance, while the Trinity indicates His three attributes (v. 213). The three hypostases of God are three attributes, also referred to as three properties and three meanings. They are neither three substances, nor three divinities, nor three gods. The term Father signifies the source of the Trinity (vv. 4-6). Elias describes the Father as the source of the substances of the Creator. From this source, the Word is generated and the Spirit proceeds. To explain his thought, Elias uses the analogy of the sun: God the Father is like the sun's disk from which light is generated and heat flows. Just as the sun with its light and heat is one, so too is the Father with His Son and Spirit one (vv. 7, 37, 39, 211-213).

Elias dedicates a large section (vv. 14-45) to explaining the relationship between God the Father and the Son. His primary concern is to avoid any materialistic interpretation of this relationship, explicitly rejecting the notion that the Son is a result of a sexual relationship. The Qur'ān in 5:116 considers the Trinity as the Father, the Son, and Mary, and consequently, in 72:3 rejects the teaching that God had a female partner with whom He produced a son. To address this misunderstanding, Elias uses the method of analogy to explain the eternal generation of the Son. He states that the Word is generated from the Father in the same way that our word is generated from the human substance and the ray is generated from the sun. Due to this type of generation the Word is called Son (v. 37).

Elias explains his thought using further analogies: just as the human word comes from the source of one's substance and takes the form of letters and words on paper, remaining inseparable from its source, and just as the sun's ray is generated from the sun's disk and extends from the sky to the earth without being separated from its origin, so too is the Word of God, generated from the source of His substance and remains inseparable from Him (vv. 38-39).

Elias additionally asserts that the Word of God is one (v. 18) and that

He is in God as the instinct of speech is in the human nature (v. 19). Consequently, he affirms, again using the method of analogy, that just as human beings are rational from the time of their creation, also God is rational from eternity, i.e., He has His Reason from eternity, and His Reason is His Word (v. 23). God has never lacked rationality (vv. 33-34). Elias explains that just as what is from the human substance is human, what is from the substance of water is water, and what is from the substance of fire is fire, so what is from the substance of God is, without doubt, God (vv. 24-25). Through these syllogisms, Elias aims to demonstrate that the Word of God is indeed God.

Using syllogisms and analogies as methods in controversial literature was very common not just among Muslim scholars, jurists, philosophers, and theologians, but also in apologetical Arabic Christian treatises and those composed in controversy with Muslims.[17] This indicates that our author, in writing the Trinitarian material of his *Commentary*, had Muslims and their understanding of the Trinity in mind. He could not have been addressing his Christian opponents, since, as he openly declares, all Christians agree on the Trinitarian dogma.[18] This is further demonstrated by his consideration of the Word of God as an essential divine attribute, a property of the substance of God, using a modified version of the Islamic doctrine on the attributes of God.

To better explain this doctrine, Elias again uses natural analogies (vv. 26-31) related to those used in his previous syllogisms regarding the water and the fire. He states that the substance of water is coldness and moisture, and the substance of fire is light and heat. Affirming that the water is cold and moist means it inherently possesses the properties of coldness and moisture. The same applies to fire, which inherently possesses the properties of lighting and heating. Additionally, in each case, these properties indicate the same substance; they are substantial, essential, and not accidental. For Elias, water is not truly water without its properties of coldness and moisture, just as fire is not truly fire without its properties of lighting and heating.

Being based on these natural analogies and syllogisms, Elias develops his Trinitarian doctrine and states: The Word is eternal in the essence of God and exists in His substance. The Word is the Father's instinct of speech, His rationality, i.e., His reason and His wisdom. Consequently,

God has eternally possessed the property of rationality and is described as being rational from eternity. Rationality is not an addition to God but is essential and substantial (vv. 32-35, 67, 204-213).

Elias uses a similar mechanism when discussing the Holy Spirit, referring again to the analogy of the sun's disk. The Spirit flows from the Father as heat flows from the sun's disk. The Spirit has the characteristic of being life-giving, and because of this, God is described as Living. This means that the property of living and life-giving is also essential and substantial in God. The Holy Spirit, moreover, is adjoined to the Holiest, meaning that the attribute of being Holy is inherent in the substance of God. Thus, God is described and called as the Holiest (v. 206).

For Elias, the divine properties, also called attributes, are essential and substantial. This means that they are nouns by which the substance of God is described. Without them the divine substance is imperfect. Elias is capable of affirming the following triads: "God is Rational and Living" and "God has Reason (Word, Wisdom) and Life". For him, both sentences are equivalent, as he understands that God is Rational through His Reason and is Living through His Life.

In Islamic thought, one of the essential attributes of God is rationality, which is related to His being wise. For the Sunnah among Muslims, God is wise by means of a Wisdom, an entity in Him. The Sunnah applies this reasoning to all the essential divine attributes.[19] It is evident how Elias uses this Sunnah thought regarding the divine attributes and employs it in his Trinitarian explanation, limiting the attributes' number to three, and calling them with the technical term property, not used by Muslim theologians.

By aligning his Trinitarian doctrine with the familiar Islamic concept of divine attributes, Elias effectively bridges the theological gap and makes the Christian understanding of the Trinity more accessible to a Muslim audience. These methods for explaining the Trinitarian doctrine are not only present in Elias's *Commentary* but also in his *Book of Demonstrations*' chapter on the Trinity and in his *First Session*, where he answers to the vizier's critiques of the Nicene Creed. This again confirms that the Trinitarian material in the *Commentary*, as well as some of its Christological arguments, were written as an apology directed towards Muslims.

6. Conclusion

In a letter written to his brother Abū Saʿīd ʿĪsā Ibn Manṣūr Elias of Nisibis sets forth a principle to be followed in dialogue: always use language that is understandable to the other party in the discussion. In his *First Session* with al-Maghribi, Elias emphasizes that if the questions and doubts of the Muslim scholar are aimed at genuinely comprehending the Christian doctrine as Christians themselves understand it, they are welcome, otherwise, it is better not to dispute or discuss. The Vizier replied to him underscoring that the condition for seeking knowledge and clarification is to ask questions and raise objections; otherwise, dialogue would become a monologue.[20]

The *Commentary on the Creed* is thus to be regarded as a concrete example of how Elias applies and employs all these principles of dialogue. He does so to answer his adversaries' questions and to defend his faith from misunderstandings and even false accusations, using accepted methods and comprehended language by his opponents.

Notes

1 On Elias, his context, writings and teaching see Bishara Ebeid, Elias of Nisibis, The Book of the Demonstration of the correctness of the faith, Critical edition, translation, introduction and comments, Cordoba: UCOPress-Èditions de l'USJ, 2023, 5-22, while for his Commentary see Bishara Ebeid, Elias of Nisibis, Commentary on the Creed, Critical edition, translation, introduction and comments, Cordoba: UCOPress-Èditions de l'USJ, 2018.
2 For a critical edition of the Book of Sessions see Nicolai Seleznyov, Liber sessionum sive disputatio inter Eliam metropolitam Nisibenum et vezirum Abū 'l-Qāsim al-usayn ibn ʿAlī al-Maġribī, Moscow: Institute for Oriental and Classical Studies, 2018.
3 Seleznyov, Liber sessionum, 10.
4 See for example Gabriel Reynolds, A Muslim Theologian in the Sectarian Milieu: ʿAbd al-Jabbār and the Critique of Christian Origins, Leiden-Boston. Brill, 2004, 163 175, while for an example of a Muslim critique against Nicaea and its Creed see Marek Nasiłowski and Diego Sarrió Cucarella, "Medieval Muslim polemics against the Christian creed: the critique of Salih b. al-Husayn al-Ga farī (d. 668/1270)," Islamochristiana 42 (2016), 71-102.
5 In regards see Neal Robinson, Christ in Islam and Christianity. The Representation of Jesus in the Qur'an and the Classical Muslim Commentaries, New York: Palgrave Macmillan, 1991.
6 Seleznyov, Liber sessionum, 31-32.
7 In regards see Samir Kh. Samir, "Entretien d'Élie de Nisibe avec le vizir al-Maġribī sur l'Unité et la Trinité," Islamochristiana 5 (1979), 31-39.

8 Ebeid, Demonstration, 53-73.
9 Ebeid, Demonstration, 160-165; Bishara Ebeid, La Tunica di al-Masī. La Cristologia delle grandi confessioni cristiane dell'Oriente nel X e XI secolo, 2nd edition, Rome: Valore Italiano-Edizioni Orientalia Christiana, 2019, 422-426.
10 Ebeid, Demonstration, 234-237.
11 Ebeid, Demonstration, 310-315.
12 For the Biblical quotations in the Commentary and their use see Ebeid, Commentary, 46-50.
13 From now on, references to the Commentary's text will be indicated by the numbers of the verses (v./vv.) of the edition.
14 On the genre of the Commentaries in Christian literature, and mainly among Arab Christians see Ebeid, Commentary, 34-35.
15 For mor details on the Commentary's Syriac text of the Creed and its Arabic translation, as well as the rest of the Arabic versions of the Creed etc., see Ebeid, Commentary, 37-46.
16 For the Trinitarian doctrine of Elias in his theological writings see Ebeid, La Tunica, 451-481.
17 For the use of analogies, syllogisms and tirades in Christian Arabic Literature see Michał Sadowski, The Trinitarian Analogies in the Christian Arab Apologetic Texts (750-1050), Cordoba: UCOPress -Èditions de l'USJ, 2019; while for their use among Muslim scholars and theologians see Sarah Stroumsa, "Logic as Interconfessional Weapon in the Early Islamicate World: Manṭiq, Qiyās, Kalām," Journal of Eastern Christian Studies 72 (2020), 181-201.
18 Ebeid, Demonstration, 104 □107.
19 In regards see for example Harry Wolfson, The Philosophy of the Kalam, Cambridge-Massachusetts-London: Harvard University Press, 1976, 112-232; see also Ebeid, Commentary, 53-54.
20 For the advice to his brother see Samir Kh. Samir, "Un traité nouveau d'Elie de Nisibe sur le sens des mots Kiyan et Ilah," Parole de l'Orient 14 (1987), 109-153, here 112; while for dialogues principles in the First Session see Seleznyov, Liber sessionum, 11.

Introducing Trinity and avoiding Trimūrti: The reception of the Trinitarian doctrine of the Nicene-Constantinopolitan Creed in Early Modern India

PAOLO ARANHA

Striking similarities between Christianity and Hinduism were noticed by Europeans since the early modern time, and are confirmed even by today's religious practice. Since the sixteenth century missionaries believed that the Christian Trinity and the Hindu Trimūrti of Brahmā, Viṣṇu and Śiva might be somehow related. This article presents various interpretations that were given for such a supposed analogy, hence assuming that the Trimūrti was either a relic or a prefiguration of Christianity, or alternatively a diabolic mockery of it. Furthermore, the article shows how a ritual object with a ternary structure hinting at Trimūrti was resignified so as to indicate Trinity.

Christianity and Hinduism: A danger or an opportunity?
It would be both simplistic and misleading to assume that the limited presence of Christianity in India (estimated in a range between 2% and 5%) may be due to a fundamental incompatibility with the general spiritual orientation of the country. In fact, reasons for such a relatively modest impact should be rather attributed to other factors, considering that Christianity in general, and possibly Roman Catholicism in a special way (amounting to at least one third of all Indian Christians), have been perceived in local contexts as strikingly similar in many aspects

to Hinduism, the most widespread religious tradition of medieval and modern India.[1] Visual evidence supporting this claim can be, for instance, the crowds of Hindu (but also Muslim) pilgrims flocking to the Marian shrine of Vailankanni, on the Coromandel coast of Tamil Nadu.[2] Such an attractiveness of a Catholic shrine for non-Christians is not an exclusive feature of rural India. For instance, "throughout Mumbai, Wednesday evening is an occasion of popular worship that brings non-Christians into the company of Christians to celebrate Novena".[3] Centre of this devotion is the Church of Saint Michael in Mahim, where special veneration is offered to an image of Our Lady of the Perpetual Succour, copied from the original Byzantine icon conserved in a church in Rome. The similarity between the Blessed Virgin and a Hindu female divinity can even be marked by verbal assonance, as in the Tamil case of *Māriyamman*, a goddess of smallpox, and *Mariyamman*, namely "Mother Mary".[4] Analogies between Roman Catholicism and Hinduism can be detected in religious practices, like pilgrimages (*tīrthayātrā*-s), as well as in sacred objects, such as holy water (*tīrtha*). Hindus attending Masses are reminded constantly by priests that the Eucharist is reserved to Catholics in grace of God, and should not be equated to the Hindu *prasāda*, namely consecrated food, first offered to deities in temples, and then distributed and partaken by all the devotees, with no regard to their official religious allegiance. In this case, the similarity between the Eucharist and the *prasāda* can even lead, from a Roman Catholic perspective to a desecration of the sacrament through its unworthy reception. At any rate, the functional differences between Eucharist and *prasāda* are not always clear, as the latter "is also said to incorporate the substance of the god, so that the worshipper is, as in the Christian Eucharist, eating God".[5] A dynamic of both similarity and distinction between Eucharist and *prasāda* is perceived even among the Khrist Bhaktas, a community of non-baptised devotees of Christ that has emerged in the Hindu holy city of Varanasi (Banaras) since the 1990s, as consequence of the efforts made by Catholic missionaries. Among the Khrist Bhaktas a clear distinction is drawn between the *prasāda* they can partake of, consisting concretely in blessed sweet buns, and the *paramprasāda* ("highest *prasāda*"), namely the Eucharist, consecrated by Catholic priests and reserved only to baptised faithful, which is "believed to be invested with divine power and thus healing properties".[6]

Similarities between Christianity and Hinduism can be verified not only at a material and practical level, but also in the realm of theological concepts. In the early modern epoch, a particularly striking case was the perceived assonance between the fundamental Christian belief in Trinity, as spelled out in the Niceno-Constantinopolitan Creed and in other professions of Faith, and the Hindu concept of Trimūrti. The latter, literally meaning "three forms" (*Tri* + *mūrti*) is believed to have emerged around the beginning of the Christian era, as a way to conceptualise the relation between the creation, the conservation and the destruction of the universe, associated respectively with the gods Brahmā, Viṣṇu and Śiva. However, the Trimūrti is not a very common object of representation and worship. Nonetheless, when the Trimūrti does occur in concrete religious practice (historical or contemporary), then either Viṣṇu or Śiva, according to sectarian divisions between vaiṣṇava and śaiva devotees, is equated with the whole Trimūrti as such. However, either Viṣṇu or Śiva are represented in this case as a single body with three heads, or even as three faces on a single head, in order to convey the idea that the very single god of choice (Viṣṇu or Śiva) is in charge of the creation, conservation and destruction of the world.[7] These basic observations are sufficient to see how the Hindu Trimūrti and the Christian Trinity emerged in entirely different religious contexts. Nonetheless, comparative theologians have not abandoned the challenge of developing creative reflections on how Trinity might be relevant in a dialogue with Hinduism. In modern times Trimūrti has ceased to be the obvious reference for such a conversation, whereas the categories of *sat* ("Being"), *cit* ("Intelligence") and *ananda* ("Bliss") have been evoked as possible Hindu counterparts to the Father, the Son and the Holy Spirit.[8] Clearly the premises for today's theological reflections are very different from the ones that dominated the Christian, and particularly the Roman Catholic interactions with Hinduism in the early modern time. Between the sixteenth and the eighteenth centuries, a reflection on the alleged similarity between Trinity and Trimūrti implied a reflection on the historical relation between Christianity and the religion of the Indian "gentiles" (*gentios* in Portuguese, *ethnici* in Latin), at a time in which the concept of "Hinduism" had not emerged yet.[9] If those "gentiles" venerated something that resembled Trinity, then Christians felt a need to relate such a devotion to their history of salvation. There were two fundamental possible interpretations, expressing respectively a moderately positive or a very negative attitude.

1) The Trimūrti might be considered as truly related to the Christian mystery of the Trinity. This positive attitude could be articulated in two scenarios, differing mostly for their respective emphasis:

a. The Trimūrti might be an enigmatic prefiguration of the doctrine of Trinity, fully disclosed only through the Christian Revelation. This approach can be compared with the long held belief in the alleged anticipation of Christian events and mysteries by pagan texts. Obvious references are the Sybilline Oracles in early and medieval Christianity.[10] In this case, emphasis was on prophecy, with the Christian revelation being the future fulfillment of those prefigurations.

b. The Trimūrti might be a relic of the one and true Faith, once widespread in India and then perverted by the superstition of the gentiles. In this second hypothesis, the remnant might either date back to some pre-Christian *prisca theologia*, or alternatively to a once widespread Christian presence in India, established by the Apostle Thomas (and possibly Bartholomew).[11] This approach can be compared to Marsilio Ficino's Christianising interpretation of the *Corpus Hermeticum*.[12] In the context of early modern Christianity in Asia, we can see here an obvious connection with the Figurism cultivated by certain French Jesuits in China between the late seventeenth and the early eighteenth century. Missionaries like Joachim Bouvet (1656-1730) or Joseph de Prémare (1666-1736) believed that the Confucian classics hinted at Christian doctrines and figures.[13] As summarised by David Mungello,

> the Figurists applied themselves assiduously to the study of ancient Chinese texts with the aim of interpreting them not as literal historical records, but as symbolical works which contained the deepest mysteries of Christianity. The Figurists argued that Chinese was a hieroglyphic script whose characters contained these secret Christian truths.[14]

In other words, in this scenario the emphasis was on antiquarian decipherment, on a remote past in which divine truth had been known, before being forgotten.

2) The Trimūrti could be considered negatively by Christians. In this case, the similarity with Trinity did not imply either an ancient prefiguration of a future Christian Revelation, or a relic of the pristine faith in the one only and true God. In this pessimistic approach, the similarity between Trimūrti and Trinity was interpreted as a satanic stratagem leading to a diabolic mockery of Truth. Theological similarity did not appear then as an opportunity for missionaries, but rather as a source of equivocation and misunderstanding, hampering the evangelisation of the gentiles. The ruse of the Devil would then consist in letting the gentiles believe that their superstitious religion and the one of the Christians were not so different: if so, why would it be necessary to convert to Christianity?

2. Early modern Christian interpretations of the Trimūrti

These two main approaches can be illustrated with concrete examples from the history of the early modern Catholic missions in India. We can find an instance of the positive attitude quite early, in a witness contemporary to Francis Xavier. It is striking that this particular observation of the Trimūrti was not even made in India, but rather in Hormuz, an island in front of the Persian port of Bandar Abbas, under Portuguese protectorate between 1515 and 1622. Here the Flemish Jesuit Kaspar Berse (or Barzæus, 1515-1543) encountered "gentile" faithful and penitents in 1549. From the context it appears how these "gentiles" were nothing but Hindus, who had settled in Hormuz for a long time. Fr. Berse believed that they had some clue (*tem rastro*) on the mystery of Trinity. He did not mention the term "Trimūrti", but it is clear that this is what he was referring to. Berse interpreted such a theological similarity as inheritance from "the philosophers": "the power of the Father, the wisdom of the Son and the goodness of the Holy Spirit".[15] Berse was clearly referring to the gymnosophists, the much renowned Indian philosophers that featured prominently in the *Alexander Romance* and in many other texts composed between the Late Antiquity and the Middle Ages.[16] We can sense how Berse's "discovery" (so to say) of the belief in the Trimūrti was a source of hope, an opportunity for evangelisation. The gentiles who had already a clue of the mystery of Trinity would have easily accepted the formulations of the Christian faith, contained in particular in the Niceno-Constantinopolitan Creed.

On the other hand, the Trimūrti appeared to many missionaries as a demonic deception. This was the claim made, for instance by the Jesuit Melchior Gonçalves in 1551 (hence just two years after Berse's positive statement), who took pride in having destroyed a temple in Vasai (near today's Mumbai) devoted to the Trimūrti. Gonçalves stressed how the gentiles wanted to deceive some ignorant people, by telling them that they too knew the mystery of the Trinity, implying that this doctrine was not an exclusive prerogative of Christianity.[17] On a similar note and in the same region, another Jesuit named Gonçalo Rodrigues, boasted in 1558 the establishment of a Christian settlement in a depopulated village where there was a sumptuous Hindu temple. Rodrigues observed how this shrine was the most remarkable example of *obra romana* ("Roman work") that he had ever seen in India.[18] This temple contained a painting of the Trimūrti, with three faces (*rostros*) on one body. Rodrigues concluded in this way: "the Devil was once very much venerated in this temple".[19]

In 1560 the Jesuit Luis Frois (1532-1587) offered a summary of the debates that the missionaries were having in Portuguese India with the Hindus about the analogies between the Trimūrti and the Trinity. The trigger for the discussion was a reflection on the meaning of the thread worn upon the left shoulder by the brahmans and the other high caste Hindus. Frois observed how this cord, called *yajñopavīta* in Sanskrit and *linha* in Portuguese, was composed of three interwoven strings, and each one of them was again formed by three other strings, fastened by a knot. The ternary structure, repeated at two different levels (almost as fractals), indicated the three divine persons, whereas the knot meant that they were a single god. With this interpretation the Hindus wanted to claim that their Trimūrti was just the same as the Christian Trinity. Furthermore, the "gentiles" explained their own Trinitarian doctrine with a natural metaphor concerning, a typical product of the land. In order to understand the argument we need to consider how this particular timber had (and still has) multiple uses in India: its powder can be employed as a pigment for drawing ritual signs (*tilaka*-s) on the forehead and other parts of the body; the wood has cosmetic and medical uses, as it is considered to be "cool" and refreshing; finally, and most obviously, sandal wood has a strong and distinctive perfume, so that it is used in the production of scents, incense sticks (*agarbattī*-s) and so on. So, according to Frois, the Hindus observed how sandalwood was one thing in itself and nonetheless it was possible to discern colour, freshness and perfume within it. Each one of these qualities was distinct, but all the three of them were found in sandalwood as a whole. However, Frois observed how such a conception was not comparable with Trinity, understood as three persons and one substance; in fact, the very term "Trimūrti" was understood (at least by Frois and the other missionaries) as implying three different gods. Furthermore, it was believed that the Hindus considered the three divinities of the Trimūrti not as co-eternal, but rather as one preceding another in time. Furthermore, it was claimed that Brahmā, Viṣṇu and Śiva were born from another supreme god, called "Parabrama". Frois was clearly referring to the concept of parabrahma, namely the Absolute or the Ultimate Reality of the Universe. It appeared clear to Frois that Trimūrti and Trinity were incomparable. Why then did the Hindus claimed that the two concepts were analogous? The Jesuit solved this perplexity by suggesting that, after the coming of the Christian missionaries, the Hindus had reinterpreted their own Trimūrti in the light of the Trinity.[20]

At the time of Frois, and still for many decades later, it was universally agreed upon that the use of signs such as the *yajñopavīta* could not be granted to the Indian neophytes, inasmuch this symbolised the pagan Trimūrti. However, after examinations undertaken by the Goa Inquisition, the General Council of the Portuguese Inquisition, and the Roman Inquisition, in 1623 eventually the Holy See granted the use of the *linha* to a specific new Christian community in India, namely to the faithful of the Madurai mission, established in 1606 by the Jesuit Roberto Nobili (1577-1656).[21] The decree *Romanæ Sedis Antistes* put an end to a conflict between missionaries and different ecclesiastical authorities, concerning the compatibility of certain customs and cultural traits with the Christian faith. At stake there was the possibility of obtaining conversions among gentiles belonging to higher castes. Among the "rites" that were essential to the maintenance of caste status by the neophytes, there was precisely the *pūnūl*, Tamil denomination of the *yajñopavīta* or *linha*. The decree allowed the use of the thread, but only as the outcome of a process of resignification:

They shall not give, receive or wear the *linea*, composed by three strings in honour, as some people say, of three gods of their nation; neither the knot by which the strings are bound… but they shall wear the linea only in memory and homage to the holy and undivided Trinity, after having recited on it a prayer to the same Most Holy Trinity, in the moment in which this *linea* is received.[22]

3. Conclusion

The similarity between the Hindu Trimūrti and the Christian Trinity could be interpreted in different ways by the missionaries and the Church authorities in the early modern time. This analogy between theological concepts was perceived variably as either an opportunity or a danger. However, beyond the interpretation of a given non-Christian belief, in a positive or negative sense, still there was space for bestowing a new meaning. Even in the case that a certain sign (such as the *yajñopavīta*) was consecrated to the "pagan" Trimūrti, it was still possible to transform the meaning of that object. Hence, even assuming that the Trimūrti was neither a prophecy nor a relic of the Trinity, but rather a diabolic mockery of it, still such a Devil's ruse was not capable of defining once for all the meaning of the signs used by a certain society. The Church, at least at the beginning of the seventeenth century, was confident in its capacity of letting the Indian neophytes transition from believing in the Trimūrti to believing in the Trinity, hence embracing the doctrine of the Niceno-Constantinopolitan and the Apostolic Creeds, without changing much in external appearances.

Notes

1 The last Census of India, held in 2011, estimated Christians to be a 2,3% of the total population. However, this seems to be a rather conservative estimate, not accounting for the wide phenomenon of the Independent Christians, not affiliated to any official church. According to Gina A. Zurlo/Todd M. Johnson (eds.), World Christian Database, Leiden/Boston: Brill, (accessed in September 2024), by 2024 the total number of Christians and all Roman Catholics were respectively 67.000.000 and 21.000.000. Since the total Indian population was estimated at 1,45 billion in 2024 (as reported in the dataset published by https://population.un.org/wpp/, consulted in September 2024), the percentage of all Christians and of the Roman Catholics at that time can be then estimated respectively as 4,6% and 1,4%.

2   See Brigitte Sébastia, Māriyamman-Mariyamman: Catholic Practices and Image of Virgin in Velankanni (Tamil Nadu), Pondichéry: French Institute of Pondicherry, 2002; Matthias Frenz, 'The Common Practice of Ritual Design in Southern India: Observations at the Marian Sanctuary of Velankanni', in Udo Simon/Christiane Brosius/Karin Polit/Petra H. Rösch/Corinna Wessels-Mevissen/Gregor Ahn (eds.), Reflexivity, Media, and Visuality, Wiesbaden: Harassowitz Verlag, 2011, 651–69. On 1 August 2024 Card. Víctor Manuel Fernández, Prefect of the Dicastery for the Doctrine of the Faith, sent a letter to the Bishop of Thanjavur, praising the devotion surrounding the shrine of Vailankanni and stressing that its popularity among non-Christians "should not be considered as a form of syncretism or mixing of religions". See "The love of Mary at Vailankanni (India)", at https://www.vatican.va/roman_curia/congregations/cfaith/documents/rc_ddf_doc_20240801_lettera-vescovo-tanjore_en.html (accessed in September 2024).
3   Marika Vicziany/Jayant Bapat, "Mumbādevī and the Other Mother Goddesses in Mumbai", Modern Asian Studies 43.2 (2009), 511–541, here 530.
4   See Sébastia, Māriyamman-Mariyamman; Anne van Voorthuizen, "Māriyamman's Śakti: The Miraculous Power of a Smallpox Goddess", in Anne-Marie Korte (ed.), Women and Miracle Stories: A Multidisciplinary Exploration, Leiden/Boston: Brill, 2004, 248-270.
5   Wendy Doniger O'Flaherty, Other People's Myths: The Caves of Echoes, New York: Macmillan, 1988, 133.
6   Kerry P. C. San Chirico, Between Hindu and Christian: Khrist Bhaktas, Catholics, and the Negotiation of Devotion in Banaras, New York: Oxford University Press 2023, 208, 214.
7   Greg Bailey, "Trimūrti" in Denise Cush/Catherine Robinson/Michael York (eds.), Encyclopedia of Hinduism, Abingdon/New York: Routledge, 2008, 886.
8   See Francis Xavier Clooney SJ, "Trinity and Hinduism", in Peter C. Phan (ed.), The Cambridge Companion to the Trinity, Cambridge: Cambridge University Press, 2011, 309-324, here 316-317.
9   On the emergence of the category of "Hinduism" see Brian K. Pennington, Was Hinduism Invented? Britons, Indians, and the Colonial Construction of Religion, New York: Oxford University Press 2005; David N. Lorenzen, Who Invented Hinduism? Essays on Religion in History, New Delhi: Yoda Press, 2009.
10 See for instance Herbert William Parke, Sibyls and Sibylline Prophecy in Classical Antiquity, edited by Brian C. McGing, London: Routledge, 1988.
11 The literature on the apostolic foundation of Indian Christianity is enormous. A critique, arguing that Christianity was established in India only in Late Antiquity has been offered by Nathanael J. Andrade, The Journey of Christianity to India in Late Antiquity: Networks and the Movement of Culture, Cambridge: Cambridge University Press, 2018.
12 See for instance Sebastiano Gentile/Carlos Gilly, Marsilio Ficino e il ritorno di Ermete Trismegisto: Marsilio Ficino and the Return of Hermes Trismegistus, Firenze: Centro Di, 1999.
13 See Claudia von Collani, Die Figuristen in der Chinamission, Frankfurt am Main: Lang, 1981; Knud Lundbæk, Joseph De Prémare, 1666-1736, S.J.: Chinese Philology and Figurism, Aarhus: Aarhus University Press, 1991; David E. Mungello, The Silencing of Jesuit Figurist Joseph de Prémare in Eighteenth-Century China, Lanham, MD: Rowman & Littlefield, 2019.

14 David E. Mungello, Curious Land: Jesuit Accommodation and the Origins of Sinology, Stuttgart: Franz Steiner Verlag, 1985, 310.
15 "Tem rastro da Trindade, o qual me parece que lhe ficou dos philosophos: a potencia do Padre e sapientia do Filho e ha bondade do Espritu Sancto". Kaspar Berse SJ to his confreres in India and Europe, from Hormuz on 10 December 1549, published by Josef Wicki SJ, Documenta Indica, Roma: Monumenta Historica Societatis Iesu, vol. 1, 639-698, here 684.
16 See recently Chiara Di Serio, Alessandro e i Brahmani: La costruzione di un'alterità ideale dalla Grecia antica al Medioevo, Roma: Bulzoni, 2024.
17 Melchior Gonçalves SJ to his Jesuit confreres in Portugal, from Cochin on 20 and 23 January 1551, published by Wicki (ed.), Documenta Indica, 1950, vol. 2, 183-185, here 184. On the life of Melchior Gonçalves, see Georg Schurhammer SJ, Francis Xavier: His Life, His Times; translated by M. Joseph Costelloe SJ, Roma: The Jesuit Historical Institute, 1980, vol. 3, 501, fn. 47.
18 The expression obra romana recurs also in other mid-sixteenth-century Portuguese descriptions of Hindu architecture and has been interpreted as a reference to sculptures in high relief or bas-relief. See Sylvie Deswarte-Rosa, "Antiquité et nouveaux mondes: A propos de Francisco de Holanda", Revue de l'art 68.1 (1985), 55-72, here 67. However, we may wonder whether obra romana indicated in this context an architecture employing arches and not merely architraves.
19 Gonçalo Rodrigues SJ to his Jesuit confreres in Portugal, from Vasai on 5 September 1558, published by Wicki (ed.), Documenta Indica, 1956, vol. 4, 96-105, here 99-100.
20 Luis Frois to his confreres in Portugal, from Goa on 8 December 1560, published by Wicki (ed.), Documenta Indica, 1956, vol. 4, 786-809, here 803-804.
21 On Roberto Nobili and the foundation of the Madurai mission see Peter R. Bachmann, Roberto Nobili, 1577-1656: Ein missionsgeschichtlicher Beitrag zum christlichen Dialog mit Hinduismus, Roma: Institutum Historicum S. I., 1972; Augustine Saulière SJ, His Star in the East, edited by Savarimuthu Rajamanickam SJ, Madras: De Nobili Research Institute, 1995; Ines G. Županov, Disputed Mission: Jesuit Experiments and Brahmanical Knowledge in Seventeenth-century India, New Delhi: Oxford University Press, 1999.
22 The decree Romanæ Sedis Antistes can be consulted in Raffaele De Martinis (ed.), Iuris Pontificii de Propaganda Fide Pars Prima, Romæ: Ex Typographia Polyglotta S. C. de Propaganda Fide, 1838, 15-17. The translation from Latin is mine.

What does Nicaea have to do with Manila? A Theological Gap and the Development of a Local Christology

AUSTIN JOHN MILLARES ORTINERO

The article will identify a theological gap in the Philippines' reception of the Nicene-Constantinople Creed by examining three potential bases: a philosophical paradigm, a humanity-centered Christology, and a local Christological development. The third ground constructed a proposed model for understanding the development of a local Christology in the Philippine context based on three significant Christological sources. The model describes how the Christological sources developed from verbatim, kerygmatic, and contextual stages. The conclusion celebrates the universal value of the Nicene-Constantinople Creed and a Church that is fully expressed in particular cultures without being limited by it.

1. Introduction

In this article, a theological gap will be identified in the Philippines' reception of the Nicene-Constantinopolitan Creed (henceforward called the Creed). The gap is interpreted to result from three possible reasons: the lack of a Filipino philosophy that can translate the full weight of the *homoousios*, the overemphasis on the humanity of Christ, and the development of a local Christology. The reader will notice a discrepancy between the Christ of the early Christological councils and the Filipino images of Christ. As a contribution, I will construct in this article a model for understanding the development of a local Christology in the Philippine context based on three significant Christological sources. It describes how the Christological sources developed from verbatim, kerygmatic, and contextual stages. The conclusion celebrates the universal value of the Creed and a Church that is fully expressed in particular cultures without being limited by it.

2. Nicaea Christology on the Consubstantiality Clause

Jaroslav Pelikan divided Christian doctrinal development in five stages: the emergence of the Catholic Tradition (100-600), Eastern Christendom (600-1700), Medieval Theology (600-1300), Reformation (1300-1700), and Modern Culture (since 1700).[1] But even a brief perusal of the early Christological councils as convened in Nicaea, Constantinople, Ephesus, and Chalcedon spanning different eras evidenced a doctrinal development. This development is a response to theological controversies which navigated on the question of the simultaneous undivided divinity and humanity of Christ and its corresponding metaphysical and theological repercussions. Thomas Weinandy said that reaching the verge of scriptural inadequacy, the first Christological council formulated the Creed and introduced an outsourced Greek concept which is "ὁμοούσιον (*homoousion*—of the same substance or of the same being"[2] or what we will call 'the consubstantiality clause'. Weinandy intriguingly adds further that there was a story that the council Fathers had two different interpretations of the imported Greek concept. Despite this, the Nicene formulation dogmatically cemented into theology Christianity's belief in the one God. With the employment of a non-biblical Greek word, Christology staged a developing articulation through credal formulation as it compounded in the succeeding councils.

A seeming opposite to theological precision comes from the *Christology of the Inarticulate,* the pioneering work of Benigno Beltran. He was able to numerically survey and present an alarming 70.55 % gap or inconsistency between the doctrinally taught Christ and the popular Christ.[3] This number shows a belief that the second person of the Trinity was created by the Father. The majority of Filipinos unconsciously create a discrepancy between doctrinally confessed Christ and the popularly experienced and celebrated Christ. Beltran observed that there is a soteriological omission in the Creed. This means that when the Creed was formulated, the soteriological aspect was taken implicitly and the ontological was made explicit. In the same sense, this pattern of ontological nuancing should make its way to local Christology and do justice to the idea of consubstantiality proclaimed by Nicaea. To account for this, Beltran notes that in the early Christian communities, the salvific aspect of the Gospel has priority over the ontological aspect. The soteriological aspect is not contested, only the ontological. Like the early Christian communities, the Filipinos are convinced of the soteriological or functional dimension of Christ which is why it is not contested, but the ontological and hermeneutical which do not directly cater to their lived experiences need equal attention. Soteriology was not made explicit in the Creed because it was taken as a given of faith. Instead, Nicaea used ontological language to explicitly address the Christological controversies. The same ontology that the Council Fathers of Nicaea used to explain who Christ is, should be replicated in the development of a local Christology to establish the continuity of Tradition. There are three items that we could identify as possible reasons for this theological gap between Nicaea and Manila. The first is an unexplored philosophical tradition that could facilitate Christian theology for the Filipino context. The second is the tendency to emphasise the humanity of Christ. The third is to take into consideration the Christological development in the Philippine Church in the same way that doctrinal development is accorded to the universal Church.

3. Three Possible Grounds for this Theological Gap

Consubstantiality is foreign to Filipino minds. The Greek philosophical paradigm from which this Christological doctrine was inspired is foreign to a Filipino mind unless it is mediated in the method that Filipinos comprehend reality. To the philosophically trained, this is discernible. But without the Greek paradigm of consubstantiality, the Filipino version loses aspects of the original Greek concept. Beltran highlights that clarifying the consubstantiality clause to Filipinos requires a philosophical exploration of Filipino concepts like time and eternity. Exemplifying the Greek formula is a task that continues to challenge the universal Church particularly in their effort to comprehensively codify the weight of the consubstantiality clause in the vernacular languages. The Vatican made its guidelines regarding liturgical translations in the document *Liturgiam Authenticam*.[4] Overall, this philosophical problem could be best understood through the process of translation. Translators dealt more with the soteriological message, and less with the ontological language. It becomes a very curious case when the soteriological content is translatable but the Greek philosophy that was used to elaborate it is not. Vicente Rafael argued that the translation that took effect in the Philippines was in aid of conversion,[5] therefore it is soteriological, and not ontological. The full force of the consubstantiality clause is untranslatable, but attempts to articulate it in the vernacular, given its soteriological significance, cannot be understated. Philosophy and the lack of it has something to say with the gap that exists between what the Church desires to communicate and teach with how the people receive and understand them. While we suggest that there is a need for a philosophical system that can fully translate and comprehend the Greek formula, this paper limits itself to identifying merely the gap.

A second point that is prevalent in Filipino Christology that arguably fails to give credence to the gravity of the Nicaean formula is the overly humanized Christ. Filipino Christology is heavy on the *Santo Niño* (Infant Jesus) and the *Poong Nazareno* (an image of Christ on his knees as he carries his cross). One could not fail to ignore *the locus theologicus* that is manifesting itself in these feasts. One could argue that one of the major strengths of Filipino Christology is expressed in these feasts. However, this second point shows the disproportionate attention to the humanity of Christ that ignores the established formulation in the Creed on the oneness of being of Christ with the Father, which ultimately refers to his divinity. There have been many criticisms and arguments regarding this disbalance of attention towards the two natures of Jesus, which reminds us of the Christological controversies of the early Christian church. At present, the lack of a philosophical system which can deliver the weight of the consubstantiality clause to the Filipinos is an unexplored local philosophical-theological ground.

As a contribution to the field of systematic theology, the third point that I would like to present is the argument on Christological reception and development. The gap we have identified in the soteriological omission and the "consubstantiality clause" are considered only temporary gaps in the sense that harmonizing Christology with the local philosophies takes time. There is a dogmatic development in the universal Church as much as in local theologies. This process of Christological development is traceable in local historical events.

There are two fronts in this Christological development: the first is theological and the second is lexical (ethno-linguistic). While there are catechetical/theological sources to prove this Christological development, it was made possible through the grammar books that have been a major priority of the missionaries. Daniel Franklin Pilario, one of the contemporary prominent Filipino theologians, has argued that the (colonial) mission's method of reconfiguring the liveable space of the people (setting up towns) and their catechetical methods involved a "first act" in the process of translation.[6] On this lexical front, there was the proliferation of dictionaries and grammar books considering that there are many ethnolinguistic groups. On the theological front, we can divide these into three stages and Christological books: a verbatim stage, a kerygmatic stage, and a contextual stage. For the first stage, I propose the publication of the *Doctrina Christiana* (1593), second is the publication of the *Mahal na Passion ni Jesuchristong Panginoon Natin na Tola* (1703), and the last stage is the publication of the *Catechism of Filipino Catholics* (1997).

Comparable to the Council of Nicaea's Creed is the Philippines' Synod of Manila in 1582-86. It officially recognized and translated the Creed in Tagalog through its *Doctrina Christiana* of 1593. *Doctrina Christiana* contained the basic catholic prayers, including the Creed, written in Hispanic and the Tagalog tongue, including the now extinct local script called *baybayin*.[7] This very early method of the *Doctrina Christiana,* making the Christian faith repeatable in the language of the Filipinos to the point that they are mnemonic in nature, can be described as the verbatim stage. John N. Crossley compared the *Doctrina Christiana* with the *Gutenberg Bible* considering that these two books were the first of its kind to be printed. He narrated that after Juan de Plasencia OFM learned the Tagalog language, he started to collate catechetical guides, which were then corrected by religious orders (Augustinians, Franciscans, Jesuits, and the Dominicans) and finally approved by the Synod of Manila.[8] The lexical nuancing made by the early missionaries in the Philippines is analogous to what happened in Nicaea. The Fathers in Nicaea were trying to articulate the faith in the manner that was never formulated before. This permits us to consider that what Nicaea was resolving at surface level was lexical in nature. The theological problems, particularly the Christological and soteriological nature, needed grammatical nuancing. In the same way, the grammatical problem in the beginning of the missionary project in the Philippines was not only an issue of grammar, it was equally theological. Both were in search for the eloquence that would be able to capture the divinity and humanity of Jesus. Moreover, this article focused on Manila for the simple reason that the first Philippine version of the Creed and many prayers were first published in Tagalog, the vernacular language of Manila. It does not intend to downplay Philippine regional languages.

The second stage of this Christological development happens in the publication of the varied versions of the *Pasyon*. The *Pasyon* is a narration of the life of Jesus Christ and is not limited only to the biblical narrative of Jesus' crucifixion and death. From a Christological development perspective, the *Pasyon* became an inflection point in Philippine Christology for three reasons: it was Christologically informative, easily communicable, and socio-politically engaging. Through the *Pasyon*, Filipinos accessed the life of Jesus Christ even when the vernacularised Bible was not yet in print. While Rene Javellana would describe the *Pasyon* as a conflation or paraphrase of the Gospel,[9] because of its apocryphal elements, I would consider it as manifesting the capacity of the authors to reflect and create a living dramatic narrative for the Filipinos, and saturate the Christian communities with the life of Christ, which is why we can consider this second stage as kerygmatic. The first of these many versions is the Tagalog publication of Gaspar Aquino de Belen's *Mahal na Passion ni Jesuchristong Panginoon Natin na Tola* in 1703. According to Javellana, three more Tagalog *Pasyon* had been printed, but the 1814 *Casaysayan nang Pasiong Mahal* became the most referenced and influential, because under it, different versions from regional languages were created which until today are continued to be printed and sold during Lenten seasons.[10] Some writers associated socio-political leanings of the *Pasyon* making it meaningful and relatable to the struggle of Filipinos for liberation from social and systemic injustices. Even the life of the martyred Philippine national hero, Dr. Jose P. Rizal, was interpreted by others as Christ-like. The most prominent of this politically oriented interpretation was Reynaldo Ileto's *Pasyon and Revolution* of 1979, which many Filipino intellectuals believed to have enliven the People Power Revolution in 1986 that toppled the decade long dictatorship without spilling blood nor igniting civil violence.

The third stage of this Christological development is the Christology of the *Catechism for Filipino Catholics* of 1997 (CFC).[11] It was published in response to the *Acts and Decrees of the Second Plenary Council of the Philippines* (1992) which was headed by the late Leonardo Zamora Legaspi, the archbishop of Caceres. CFC called itself an inculturated catechism. It has three main parts: Part One: Christ, our Truth (Doctrinal), Part Two: Christ, our Way (Moral), and Part Three: Christ, Our Life (Sacraments/Worship). CFC acknowledges its roots in the Apostles' Creed and the Nicene-Constantinopolitan Creed, through which Filipinos partake in the dynamism of the living Church. The full development introduced by the CFC is presenting Christ's truth in its doctrinal, moral, and worshipping grounds. Otherwise, Filipino Christology risks itself to ritualism and idolatry. This book also identified some of the common objections against the Nicene-Constantinopolitan Creed as impersonal, abstract, formulaic, and divisive; on the contrary, CFC argues that the Creed acted as a summary of beliefs, pledge of loyalty, and a proclamation of Catholic identity. This publication of CFC is sufficient proof of the transition from rudimentary catechetical inputs of the *Doctrina Christiana* and the dramatic humanization of Christ in the *Pasyon*. Lastly, one of the major characteristics of the CFC is its contextual approach, making way for a contextualised Christology.

4. Conclusion: The Universal Value of the Nicene Creed

Lewis Ayres argues that the council fathers in Nicaea, fortified by their "local baptismal creeds," were neither conscious nor would have anticipated that their definition of the creed would be universal.[12] But 1700 years since then, after the validation of the succeeding councils of Constantinople (381), Ephesus (431), Chalcedon (451) and more, these councils were content on the readiness of Greek philosophy to give theology the ability to express what would naturally be difficult to conceptualise. I am not claiming that there is no Filipino philosophy that can bridge theology to contexts, rather that there is a gap in Filipino philosophy that can specifically translate Greek philosophy in aid of understanding the consubstantiality clause. The disparity shows that it does not mean one philosophical system is superior to the other, it means rather that there are alternatives to understanding the universality of Jesus' identity. Such interpretative alternatives are concretely manifested through contextual theologies and Christologies.

A note on the authorship of the three Christological sources shows how national ownership of Christology was happening. While the *Doctrina Christiana* was authored by foreign missionaries, and the different versions of the *Pasyon* were penned by independent natives and missionaries, the CFC was authored by the local bishops in consultation with lay and cleric experts and was granted the approval of the Holy See. CFC speaks of national pride and ownership of a faith that once only belonged and confessed in Nicaea. The Fathers of Nicaea may not have imagined that what they did would be universal. There is continuity between Nicaea and Manila, not rupture, despite a patient moment of discontinuity giving way for their Christological development. As much as there is a theological development that is measurable in mainstream theology, there is also a continuing local Christological development. One can be postcolonial or decolonial in theological method, or one can be post-Nicene, in the sense of following the succeeding councils, but one cannot be de-Nicaean. There is no escaping the positive influence of the Council of Nicaea. The effect of Nicaea in their official declaration of the formula of the catholic faith is truly universal and attempts of reinterpretation, for continuity and discontinuity purposes, are highly recommended as part of a Christological development, both locally and universally. This mysterious blend found in catholicity shows that the Church is fully expressed in culture, yet it is not limited to any culture. The Creed, both universal and local, and the theologians should be patient as this doctrinal development unfolds.

Notes

1 Jaroslav Pelikan, The Christian Tradition: A History of the Development of Doctrine, Chicago and London: The University of Chicago Press, 1971, front matters.
2 Thomas G. Weinandy, "The Doctrinal Significance of the Councils of Nicaea, Ephesus, and Chalcedon," in Francesca Aran Murphy (ed.), The Oxford Handbook of Christology, New York: Oxford University Press, 2015, 550–567, here 554.
3 Benigno P. Beltran, The Christology of the Inarticulate: An Inquiry into the Filipino Understanding of Jesus the Christ, Manila: Divine Word Publications, 1987, 77.
4 Congregation for Divine Worship and the Discipline of the Sacraments, "Liturgiam Authenticam," at https://www.vatican.va/roman_curia/congregations/ccdds/documents/rc_con_ccdds_doc_20010507_liturgiam-authenticam_en.html, [21 March 2024].

5 Vicente Rafael, Contracting Colonialism: Translation and Christian Conversion in Tagalog Society under Early Spanish Rule, Durham and London: Duke University Press, 1993, 27.
6 Daniel Franklin E. Pilario, "The Double Truth of (Colonial) Mission)," in C. Lledo Gomez et al. (eds), 500 Years of Christianity and the Global Filipino/a, Pathways for Ecumenical and Interreligious Dialogue, Switzerland: Springer Nature, 2024, 47–63, here 55.
7 "Doctrina Christiana: The First Book Printed in the Philippines, Manila, 1593" in Edwin Wolf (ed), The Project Gutenberg of Doctrina Christiana, at https://www.gutenberg.org/files/16119/16119-h/16119-h.htm, [21 March 2024].
8 John N. Crossley, "Doctrina Christiana: National Treasure, World Treasure," in The Journal of History Vol. LXII (January-December), 2016, 135–161, here 138–139.
9 Rene B. Javellana, SJ, "The Sources of Gaspas Aquino de Belen's Pasyon," Philippine Studies 32, (1984), 305-21, here 310.
10 Rene B. Javellana, SJ, "Pasyon Genealogy and Annotated Bibliography," Philippine Studies 31.4 (1983), 451-467, here 458-9.
11 Catholic Bishops' Conference of the Philippines, Catechism for Filipino Catholics, New Edition with Expanded Subject Index and Primer, Manila, Word and Life Publications, 1997, paragraphs no. 228-239.
12 Lewis Ayres, Nicaea and its Legacy: An Approach to Fourth-Century Trinitarian Theology, Oxford, Oxford University Press, 2004, 85-86.

The liturgical "decanonisation" of the Nicene-constantinopolitan Creed. Inserting the "Apostolic" Creed in the Post-Vatican II *Ordo Missae*

MASSIMILIANO PROIETTI

Before and after Vatican II a variety of rites has always corresponded to a variety of formulas used to express the Christian faith. Over the centuries, however, the Nicene-Constantinopolitan Creed had assumed a predominant role as a "liturgical" creed, due to its presence in the Liturgy of the Mass. Thus, with the liturgical reform of Vatican II, the foundational actuosa participatio *in the baptismal priesthood, and the renewed understanding of the relationship between baptism and the liturgy itself, had to correspond to a rediscovery of a 'baptismal' formula of faith to be included also in the Liturgy of the Mass: the so-called Apostles Creed.*

1. The starting-point: before and after Vatican II

During the inaugural celebration of the Second Vatican Ecumenical Council the profession of faith was solemnly made following the provisions of the *Ordo synodi*. This part of the lengthy celebration took place as follows: after the recitation of the Nicene-Constantinopolitan Creed by John XXIII kneeling at the faldistorio, the secretary of the Council, Monsignor Felici, recited the formula on behalf of all the Fathers present, who had only to declare their assent and swear loyalty to those words[1]. This was one of the acts that gave the idea of a passive participation by the bishops, spectators at a ceremony far from the expectations nourished towards the Council. In the eyes of the prominent liturgist Josef Jungmann, that celebration had demonstrated the "*terminus a quo* of liturgical matters,"[2] the necessary starting-point of the liturgical reform of Vatican II. The efforts of half-a-century of activity of the liturgical movement seemed to be in vain, as Cullman had ironically pointed out to Congar after the celebration of 11 October: "So this is your liturgical movement? But alas! It has scarcely got through the Bronze Door!"[3]

In the following decades, however, the reform initiated by the Council would change the face of the Roman liturgy. With regard to the profession of faith, it would contribute to its new appreciation, reflecting the recovery of the baptismal dimension of the liturgy and therefore of the profession of faith as a reference to baptism in which the principle of the active participation of the faithful in the liturgy on which was founded, with *Sacrosanctum concilium*. This appreciation is signified in a variety of ritual acts, all of which involve the *viva voce* participation of the celebrating assembly.

On the other hand, the relationship between liturgy and symbols of faith is historically a relationship of plurality. At the same time, at least since the liturgical reform of the Council of Trent, a unique relationship has been established between the different formulas and the different liturgical celebrations. In particular, in the context of the Eucharistic celebration, where the presence of the Creed is envisaged, it was not possible until after Vatican II that a formula other than that of the Nicene-Constantinopolitan Creed could be used. When preparing the new *Ordo Missae* there would have been a crisis from the proposal to enhance the plurality of formulas of faith, especially the Apostles' Creed. This is a text whose inclusion in the Mass should have helped to make concrete at a ritual level the theological and ecclesiological principles of *Sacrosanctum concilium*. To be definitively implemented, the proposal had to follow a more tortuous path than expected.

2. The profession of faith in the Roman liturgy: a multiplicity of formulas

The profession of faith made by the pope and Felici did not consist in its entirety of the recitation of the text of the Nicene-Constantinopolitan Creed alone, but also of the anti-Lutheran formulation promulgated by Pope Pius IV at the conclusion of the Council of Trent. The Nicene-Constantinopolitan

Creed was but the first part, followed by a series of specifications of apologetic flavour. The post-Tridentine additions represented the last piece of the elaboration of that text which, starting from the Council of Nicaea, had gradually established itself, through subsequent passages and synodal enrichments, as a canonical norm of the faith.[4] Starting at least from the Carolingian age, the Nicene-Constantinopolitan Creed had also entered the Roman liturgy and, thanks to its inclusion in the Mass, had supplanted its local competitors in fame and importance, including the so-called Apostoles' Creed.[5] This latter text had a tradition rooted in the West even before the Nicene modification, as it depended directly on the ancient symbol of the faith of the church of Rome[6]; its apostolic origin was not questioned until twentieth-century historical and philological studies. The Tridentine *professio*, declaring that the Nicene-Constantinopolitan Creed was the text of the *symbolo fidei* "Sancta Romana Ecclesia utitur", affirmed that that was the reference text of the Church of Rome. In this way, the historical process that had gradually led to the insertion of the Nicene Creed into the Western canonical and liturgical tradition was definitively sanctioned.

In the liturgical context, however, the multiplicity of ways of expressing the profession of faith remained a matter of fact, even after Trent. The post-Tridentine rubric rigidity, however, left little room for possible variations. In the rite of baptism of children the priest was expected to recite, at the beginning, the Apostoles' Creed, which was followed by the profession in interrogative form made by the godfather. Similarly, the profession of faith in an interrogative form was central to the baptism of adults, where it reflected that dynamic path between repentance – confession – profession of faith typical of the baptismal sacrament (ἐξομολόγησις), but the high point of the celebration required the catechumen to recite the Apostolic symbol, legacy of the itinerary of the catechumentate with the *traditio* and the *redditio symboli*.[7] Another particular exception was the so-called Athanasian Creed[8] within the complex *Ritus exorcizandi obsessos a daemonio*; the same Creed was used in the *Breviarium Romanum* as a hymn in the Office of Prime on Sundays. In the Mass, or rather in those celebrations of the Mass that included the profession of faith, there was no possibility of varying between these formulas and forms of profession of faith. On the contrary, the multiple rites corresponded to multiple texts, but crystallised internally in a very rigid system of rubrics, which contributed to keeping alive the main distinction between the two texts: on the one hand the more complex Nicene-Constantinopolitan text used in the Mass, and on the other the Apostoles' Creed, simpler but more ancient, now characterized as the new catechetical and baptismal formula par excellence.

This rigid distinction, however, had at least one consequence: in the life of the churches, that baptismal formula, which made its own by the faithful through catechetical instruction in vernacular languages, was not then "lived" through extensive liturgical use. In fact, in a context already foreign to the concept of *actuosa participatio* later developed in the Council, the faithful rarely had the possibility to express the profession of faith with their voice. Even when, with the gradual spread of the "dialogue" Mass during the twentieth century thanks to the Liturgical Movement, the assembly began to literally acquire a "voice" in liturgical celebrations, the profession of faith usually took place according to the text of the Nicene-Constantinopolitan Creed. This was, of course, a norm: the practice could have been different, and timid signs of the need for a change were already felt before Vatican II. One example of this is the possibility, introduced by Pius XII's reform of Holy Week (1951-1955), of making the profession of faith in the interrogative form on Easter night in the vernacular language. But not only that: when in 1964 the very famous *Misa Criolla* was composed, using the Spanish translation of the *ordinarium Missae*, it was not the Nicene-Constantinopolitan Creed, which had a long musical tradition behind it, was not chosen for the profession of faith, but rather the Apostoles' Creed. The text, known as we have noted thanks to its use in the catechetical sphere, finally also found its space within the Mass, and this choice reflected a practice already established in some communities well before the Council. The need to question the role that the Nicene text had assumed in the Roman liturgy since the Carolingian age was therefore evident. Now it was up to the liturgical reform to implement this request, which was not unrelated to two key principles of the Constitution on the liturgy: liturgical adaptation (*aptatio*) and active participation (*actuosa participatio*).

3. *Sacrosanctum concilium*: the baptismal dimension of the liturgy and its ritual expression

Recovering a baptismal dimension in the liturgy was not a meaningless operation from an ecclesiological and ecumenical point of view; on the contrary, the reflection on baptism would prove to be one of the most fruitful paths for the ecumenical movement, at least in the two decades following Vatican II.[9] Within the Liturgical Movement, however, the debate about the common priesthood of the faithful and the relationship between the exercise of this priesthood and active participation in the liturgy had already been ongoing since the start of the century. It was a theme particularly dear to some members of the conciliar Liturgical Commission and destined to become one of the most important points of the conciliar Constitution on the liturgy. In the Commission, the debate revolved around two distinct nuances[10]: on the one hand, those who identified the foundation of the active participation of the faithful in the liturgy in the common priesthood received by the faithful in baptism (Giulio Bevilacqua), and on the other, those who identified it in the baptism within an ecclesiological and liturgical conception focussed on the community dimension of the church and worship (Pierre Jounel).[11]

In its final draft, the Constitution on the liturgy leans towards the second option. The baptismal foundation of active participation in the liturgy emerges above all in nos. 6 and 14 of *Sacrosanctum concilium*: the liturgy implements the work of salvation, as through baptism the faithful are introduced to the paschal mystery of Christ of which the liturgy is a celebration (SC§6); and, by virtue of baptism itself, they have the right and duty to be formed in an *actuosa partecipatio* in the liturgy (SC§14). At the same time, the reference to 1 Pet. 2:9 in SC§6 seems to be intended to reconcile the two views.

An application of the liturgical constitution that aimed not only at a "ritual" revision but at a substantial reform of the liturgy according to the principles expressed in *Sacrosanctum concilium*, therefore, could not ignore these elements, which had to find correspondence both in euchology and in a new appreciation of baptismal elements within liturgical celebrations.

Apparently, the question was easy to resolve, and from a ritual point of view some answers could already be found in the text of the Constitution on the liturgy itself, which prescribed that the renewal of baptismal promises be included in the rite of Confirmation (SC§71), and which would also recover the baptismal (or rather, catechumenal) character of Lent by drawing on the most ancient tradition of the Church (SC§109.a). However, it was an open topic, which could not be limited to any specific case, the more so since the liturgical reform could not ignore a hermeneutics of *Sacrosanctum concilium* which went beyond the letter of the text and was implemented in the living practice of the churches.[12] In this sense, the problem of active participation coincided with that of liturgical adaptation. It is no coincidence that the same reform of the Lenten liturgy envisaged by the constitution was also hoped for by the subsequent conciliar decree *Ad gentes* (AG§14), aiming to recover the baptismal dimension.

Starting from this interpretation, we understand how the pre-conciliar liturgical practice concerning the profession of faith needed to be re-thought. The first element examined would have been, in this sense, the liturgical pre-eminence of the Nicene-Constantinopolitan Creed. If the active participation of the faithful was based in baptism, and if it was necessary to rediscover the baptismal dimension of liturgy, then one of the paths to follow was that of the baptismal formulas and, among these, the text considered baptismal par excellence: the Apostoles' Creed.

4. An unexpected arrival: the *Ordo Missae* in the post-conciliar period

Thus, the idea of combining the Nicene-Constantinopolitan Creed with the possibility of reciting the Apostolic symbol during Mass was proposed from the beginning of the work of revising the *Ordo Missae*, carried out by *coetus X* of the *Consilium ad exsequendam constitutionem de sacra liturgia* and the possibility was already included in the first schema.[13] There were different positions on this matter.

The debate revolved around three questions: a) whether it was appropriate to translate the Nicene-Constantinopolitan symbol into vernacular languages; b) if it was appropriate to place the Apostles' Creed next to it; c) in this case, if it were possible to translate it and make it possible to be sung. With regard to translation, one could not fail to take into consideration the fact that a translation into many languages was not only already available, but also memorised, through catechisms. The position of the majority of the *Consilium* was clear: precisely because of its baptismal tradition and its simplicity, the Apostles' Creed had to be adopted as an alternative to the Nicene-Constantinopolitan Creed, making the two texts equivalent within those celebrations which included the recitation of the profession of faith. However, it was Paul VI who insisted on the preservation of the Nicene Creed alone, setting his own veto on the matter[14]. The pope – who had already once blocked the work of *coetus X* in October 1965 – believed that the text of Nicaea and Constantinople was more complete from a theological and doctrinal perspective and that to renounce the pre-emience it had acquired in the Romain liturgy could have hindered, rather than strengthened, ecumenical dialogue with the Orthodox churches. However, his position not only did not take into consideration the liturgical status of the Apostoles' Creed in the churches of the Protestant and Reformed tradition, but did not even consider the practice already established in the local churches.

This was no small matter. The status and text of the profession of faith in the liturgy already represented relevant issues in themselves; to this was added the fact that the use of the Apostoles' Creed brought with it a consolidated tradition of vernacular use, with all that this entailed in the context of a heated debate on the *status* of Latin in the Roman liturgy. The question, marginal for some, was particularly significant for those bishops who, especially outside European borders, eagerly awaited the moment to put into practice the content of the constitution regarding liturgical adaptation. The veto placed by Paul VI was circumvented by the decision taken at the 1967 synod to allow episcopal conferences to adopt it locally. The result was that the Apostoles' Creed, absent from the 1969 *Ordo Missae* and from the 1970 first *editio typica* of the Roman Missal, nevertheless appeared in the majority of national editions of the conciliar Missal. The univocal relationship between the Creed of Nicaea and Constantinople and the liturgy of the Mass was therefore undermined.

This was a decisive step, not only for the centrality played by the Eucharist in the liturgical life of the churches, but also because it opened up the way to a multiplicity of formulas often not traced by the liturgical books. In fact, the recovery of the "baptismal" formula of the Apostoles' Creed is also accompanied, in the practice of communities, by a new life of those professions of faith made in an interrogative form and even more easily "adaptable"; formulas that more immediately recall the baptismal dimension. Thus began a process of "liturgical decanonisation" of the Nicene-Constantinopolitan Creed, which went hand-in-hand with more general questioning about it based not on its content but rather on the text itself and on the indelible imprint of Greek philosophy that it brought with it. This development was on the same level as what was done, on the theological side, by Karl Rahner, with the elaboration of the three "short formulas", which, not by chance, refer to the Apostoles' Creed for its simplicity[15]. Rahner's work is based on the idea that in the context of theological pluralism, the unity of the profession of faith was not guaranteed by the text itself but rather by the expression and celebration, in the liturgy, of the content of that text.[16]

The success of the possibility of alternating, in local practice, the Nicene-Constantinopolitan Creed and the "baptismal" symbol of the Apostles is demonstrated by the fact that, thirty years later, the last Latin *editio typica* of the *Missale Romanum* (2002) acknowledged this possibility. In fact, regarding the profession of faith, the norm states: "Instead of the Nicene-Constantinopolitan Creed, especially during Lent and Easter Time, the baptismal Symbol of the Roman Church, known as the Apostles' Creed, may be used". From an historical and philological point of view, of course, the rubric is not strictly correct, as it constructs an overlap between the so-called Apostoles' Creed and the ancient baptismal creeds of the church of Rome. Furthermore, compared to the practice of the communities, which is certainly difficult to trace, reception remains partial, not contemplating the possibility of using other methods of profession of faith, such as those in interrogative form widespread in many communities.

Nonetheless, that norm represents the anchoring of a debate and the reception of a request, that of a greater liturgical appreciation of this "baptismal" formula, coming not only from scholars and experts, but also from local communities. In presenting this new *editio typica*, this passage was highlighted and justified with two reasons[17]: the authority give to the Apostoles' Creed by its antiquity and the fact that in the majority of missals in the national languages the text was already present and widely used; an already consolidated practice was therefore implemented. Consolidated, of course, because it allowed the relationship between baptism and liturgy to be further highlighted, especially in certain periods of the liturgical year; but also consolidated because the adoption in the *Ordo Missae* of that text, used for centuries for catechesis and already widespread and memorised, before Vatican II, in its vernacular translation, represented a further step within that process of returning to the People of God its own *lex orandi* initiated by the Liturgical Movement and definitively sanctioned by *Sacrosanctum concilium*.

Translated by Patricia Kelly

Notes

1 AS 1/1, 156–158.
2 Josef Andreas Jungmann, Konzilstagebuch, 11 October 1962; the typescript of the diary is kept at the Innsbruck University Institut für Liturgiewissenschaft and there is a copy at Bologna Foundation for Religious Studies.
3 Yves Congar, Mon journal du Concile, ed. Éric Mathieu: Volume 1, Paris: Cerf, 2002, 112.
4 Giuseppe L. Dossetti, Il simbolo di Nicea e di Costantinopoli: Edizione critica, Rome-Freiburg: Herder, 1967; John N. D. Kelly, Early Christian Creeds, 3rd edition, London: Longman, 1972, 62–99, 205–367; Costanza Bianchi/Alberto Melloni (eds.), The Creed of Nicaea (325): Status Quaestionis and the Neglected Topics, Göttingen : Vandenhoeck & Ruprecht, 2024; Wolfram Kinzig, A History of Early Christian Creeds, Berlin: De Gruyter, 2024.
5 Enrico Cattaneo, Il culto cristiano in Occidente: Note storiche, Rome: Edizioni Liturgiche, 1978, 184–200; Bernard Capelle, "Alcuin et l'histoire du symbole de la messe", Recherches de théologie ancienne et médiévale 6 (1934), 249–260.
6 Kelly, Early Christian Creeds, 368–434; Wolfram Kinzig, Das Apostolische Glaubensbekenntnis: Leistung und Grenzen eines christlichen Fundamentaltextes, Berlin-Boston: De Gruyter, 2018.
7 Victor Saxer, Les rites de l'initiation chrétienne du IIe au VIe siècle: Esquisse historique et signification d'après leurs principaux témoins, Spoleto: Centro Italiano di Studi sull'Alto Medioevo, 1988.
8 John N. D. Kelly, The Athanasian Creed, London: Adam & Charles Black, 1964.
9 Dagmar Heller, Baptized into Christ: A Guide to the Ecumenical Discussion on Baptism, Geneva: WCC Publications 2012; Luca Ferracci, Battesimo Eucaristia Ministero. Genesi e destino di un documento ecumenico, Bologna: Il Mulino, 2021.
10 Angelo Lameri, Alla ricerca del fondamento teologico della partecipazione attiva alla liturgia: Il dibattito nella commissione preparatoria del Concilio Vaticano II, Rome: CLV, 2016.
11 A copy of the documentation about this is in the archive of the Foundation for Religious Sciences in Bologna, Vatican Council II series, Fondo Bevilacqua, fasc. 10–13 and Fondo Jounel, fasc. 8. The original documentation is respectively at the Oratorio della Pace in Brescia and in the Centre de Pastoral Liturgique in Paris.
12 Giuseppe Dossetti, Per una chiesa eucaristica: Rilettura della portata dottrinale della costituzione liturgica del Vaticano II, Lezioni del 1965, eds. Giuseppe Alberigo/Giuseppe Ruggeri, Bologna: Il Mulino, 2002.
13 Maurizio Barba, La riforma conciliare dell'Ordo Missae. Il percorso storico-redazio-

nale dei riti d'ingresso, di offertorio e di comunione, Roma: CLV, 2002. Some schema attesting to this phase are in Archives Martimort (Institut Catholique de Toulouse, *Archives Martimort*, Vc20/6 ; Vc21/7).

14 Annibale Bugnini, La riforma liturgica (1948-1975), 2ª edizione, Rome: CLV, 1997, 335–389; 356 nota 21.
15 Karl Rahner, Grundkurs des Glaubens: Einführung in den Begriff des Christentums, Freiburg: Herder, 1976, 435–440.
16 Karl Rahner, "Der Pluralismus in der Theologie und die Einheit des Bekenntnisses in der Kirche", Concilium 6 (1969), 125–147.
17 The intervention of the then Secretary of the Congregation for Divine Worship and Discipline of the Sacraments, Francesco Pio Tamburrino, in the section dedicated to the Bulletins of the Holy See Press Office of the vatican.va website, Bulletin B0150 of 22/03/2002.

The Nicene-Constantinopolitan Creed in the editions of *Communio* (1972-1975). A struggle for Catholic identity?

GUISEPPE SAMUELE ADORNO

After briefly presenting some of the most relevant developments of Catholic fundamental theology in the post-conciliar period, particularly in relation to the Trinitarian theology implied by the Nicene Creed, this article aims to critically present how these developments were attacked in the pages of the newly-founded journal Communio between 1972 and 1975. The ample space reserved for reflection on the Nicene-Constantinopolitan Creed by the various national editions of the journal, in fact, testifies to the tensions and concerns about the "de-Hellenisation" of the Christian faith; the controversy, for which this article simply intends to reconstruct a significant stage, would lead to the harsh "defence of the faith" policy of the 1980s and 1990s.

1. Paul VI and the "crisis of faith"

By implicitly abrogating many previous teachings (for example, on religious freedom), the Second Vatican Counciul had given the Catholic Church a sound awareness of the relativity of many of its doctrines. This gave room to open reflection within which to re-think the reality and formulas of faith and the Christian experience from their foundations.

This questioning did not fail to also touch the substance of the articles of the Nicene-Constantinopolitan Creed; this movement was based on a renewed historical-critical reading of the founding traditions and of the concrete experience of being church *within* (and not *against*) contemporary society. A new generation of theologians, represented above all by the Concilium group, intended to pursue in a more radical manner the *ressourcement* adopted by the Council with regard to post-Tridentine scholasticism, and to return to the source of the Gospel beyond the medieval mediations and, in the case of the Creed, the patristic mediations.

From 1964 the Holy See reacted against this spiritual and theological movement, interpreting it under the sign of "crisis"; in his catecheses and speeches, Pope Paul VI often showed himself to be concerned about relativism and the supposed contempt for dogmas which were spreading in the Catholic Church, and the Congregation for the Doctrine of the Faith began processes against both individual theologians and pastoral experiments such as the Dutch Catechism (1966-67), accused of fuelling the general "confusion". The Credo of the People of God, pronounced by the pope on behalf of all the faithful on 30 June 1968, on the occasion of the celebration at the end of the Year of Faith, must be placed in this climate of suspicion and tension[1]. In essence, it is a long paraphrase of the Nicene-Constantinopolitan Creed interpolated with articles of faith deriving from later and specifically Catholic dogmas[2].

From the introduction, the proclamation does not argue or demonstrate, but affirms and professes; it does not dialogue, but implicitly condemns. By highlighting the immutable stability not only of the contents of the faith, but also of the words to express them, it intends to protect the "faith of the simple", thrown into doubt by the spread of a materialist worldview, and to disavow the progress of contemporary theological science, which, going through a "paradigm shift", was re-thinking faith from its foundations.

2. The international theological journal *Communio*. A "campaign for the Creed" (1972-1975)?

Many people saw the editorial project of *Communio* as the ideological counterpart of the intellectual movement represented by the journal *Concilium*; the two journals often serve as labels to create a division between two fields of Catholic theological research, and this binary reading has influenced post-conciliar historiography. Although simplistic, this approach is not devoid of elements of truth; but having admitted the reality of the ideological polarisation represented by the two journals, what are the reasons that led theologians such as de Lubac, von Balthasar and Ratzinger to leave the editorial staff of *Concilium*? Around which themes did the controversy focus most?

An initial part of the response can be ascertained by examining the editions from the first years of *Communio*. For the most part, the authors address issues related to the so-called crisis of faith, dedicating themselves to a true spiritual and theological apologia of the Catholic faith in its classical form, patristic and medieval.

In this regard, the many contributions that were dedicated to reflection on the Creed are of particular relevance: several times already in the early years of the Italian and German editions[3]; after the American edition managed to establish a quarterly rhythm in 1974, with the edition *On Christology*, in which some articles explicitly took up the Christological articles of the Nicene Creed[4]; then, in the Italian and German editions, the first edition of 1975 was exclusively dedicated to the Creed[5]; finally, the first issue of the French edition, published in September of the same year 1975, bore the significant title "la confession de la foi"[6].

2.1 Vis-à-vis controversies and main themes

What does the "defence of the Creed" that emerges from all these articles of the various issues of *Communio* between 1972 and 1975 share? What general trends can be detected? Without having the opportunity here to go into detail about the individual contributions mentioned in the previous paragraph, we will limit ourselves to listing some of the recurring elements.

The authors often refer to a "confessing" practice of theology, based on the first-person spiritual experience of prayer and profession of faith, which assigns to God the role of *subject* and not *object* of intellectual research. The prose of the texts themselves goes beyond the scientific approach of the theological articles, and often indulges in dramatic and existential tones; several pages of the journal are pleased with the mystical undertones and sometimes a "prayerful" style; for example, de Lubac delves into a profession of faith in the form of an "anti-Gnostic Creed"[7]. This attitude is often accompanied by an outright condemnation of contemporary theologians, said to be too independent and intellectualistic, disconnected from the living body of the Church and not centred on an authentic experience of faith.

Then, the "objective" reality of the articles of faith and their essentially "vertical" nature are constantly emphasised. It is precisely the profound unity and co-implication of vertical and horizontal instances (necessarily in this order) that, according to the *Communio* team, theologians seduced by secularised thought would not be able to grasp. A selectivity is therefore repeatedly denounced which is incapable of holding together the polar binomials which in dynamic tension together constitute the deepest mysteries of the Christian faith. This criticism almost becomes a recurring *Denkfigur*: the *aut-aut*s advanced by modern reason to give meaning to faith are contrasted with the *et-et*s whose polar tension would find a unifying resolution in the mystery of divine action in history. Thus according to the theologians of *Communio*, faith and orthodoxy are not a threat to the radicality of charity and orthopraxy, but rather constitute their necessary condition: rejecting the Creed would be equivalent to rejecting the communion of love in Christ which can only be established *through* and *within* the Church. The same goes for many other paradoxical *et-et*: postulating the objective essence of God as the foundation of reality does not prevent us from recognising him in his "economic" giving of himself for the salvation of humanity; *believing in* God, that is, completely entrusting oneself to him (*fides qua*), necessarily presupposes *believing that* God exists, and believing in his Word (*fides quae*)[8]; in this adherence to God one cannot distinguish faith and religion, personal and objective; Christ's divinity is not a threat to the reality of his humanity; the uniqueness of the fact of the Incarnation as the supreme and definitive Revelation of the triune God does not detract from the importance of other religious experiences, which indeed would fully reveal their meaning and role around the centre represented by Christ[9].

The same desire to integrate radically different requests (easy to claim on a spiritual level, but difficult to translate into concrete requests) also emerges with respect to the question posed by the "short formulas of faith": are these attempts to present the faith with words understandable to the contemporary man or woman to be preferred to ancient formulas, which in their essentialism are often perceived as abstract and of little relevance? For the theologians of *Communio* the question is poorly posed: we must strive to find new formulas, suitable for the ever-changing contexts with which the Church will come into contact, but without relativising the ancient symbols, which guard the heart of Christian doctrine. This underlies a series of clear stances at a theological level: a notion of

Tradition that allows additions but not replacements; a clear distinction between doctrinal and pastoral; a pneumatology such that the Spirit has the task of "remembering" and "deepening" the Revelation of Christ, but cannot suggest anything *new*; a very high conception of the synthesis of faith carried out by the Fathers according to the Greek philosophical categories, considered "foundational"[10]; a minimalist understanding of the magisterium of *Gaudet Mater Ecclesia*.

Several of the issues taken into consideration strive to fill the *gap* highlighted by contemporary historical-critical exegesis, which revealed how the Trinitarian doctrine formulated in Nicaea could not be easily superimposed on the pluralism of New Testament Christologies. In short, the aim is to demonstrate that the Trinity is an indispensable prerequisite for an understanding of the Gospels, and to argue for its exegetical and spiritual plausibility. This goes hand-in-hand with an effort to counter the process of "demythologisation" invoked and pursued by several contemporary theologians and exegetes.

In particular, in the issue explicitly dedicated to the Creed, the initial position of pre-eminence reserved for the Father is greatly emphasised. Denouncing (without naming names) the anthropocentric theological projects of those who would like to start from a Spirit understood as a libertarian inspiration to reinvent nature, or from a Son seen as a perfect man, Hegelian teleology of aspirations and of the individual and of society, de Lubac and Ratzinger reiterate the pre-eminence that the Creed gives to the works of creation, thus orienting everything that follows: Jesus is the Son par excellence, he receives his entire being *from another*; the Spirit is the one who reminds the faithful of their creatureliness and keeps them in obedience to the Father. In his contribution, Ratzinger deduces the ethical consequences of this approach: "at this point the alternative posed by the first article of faith becomes clear: it is a question of knowing whether man accepts reality as purely material or as the expression of a sense that concerns him; whether he must invent or find values. Depending on his decision, he is dealing with two completely different freedoms"[11]. The Christian would not have the freedom to *devise* justice, but to *correspond* to it. Other articles in the issue (e.g., Milano, Ulrich) emphasise this aspect: the loss of the creaturely condition and of the original sense of authority would have to do with the crisis of the figure of the father in contemporary society. This theological understanding of Creation is deeply linked to a notion of "nature" that would influence the developments of the sexual morality of the Catholic Church in the following decades.

2.2 Different styles of controversy
Nearly all the articles we have considered have a controversial nature. However, the intensity of the controversy, the style and the strategies used differ greatly from author to author. For example, Klaus Reinhardt very precisely presents the theories of some of the proponents of "Christology from below", highlighting their positive traits and taking care to defend them from trivialisations and misunderstandings. Louis Bouyer, on the other hand, tends to present the theses of his "progressive" opponents in a distorted and extreme way, and to criticise them in an even more rhetorical and dramatic way (to the point of arguing that those "of today" do not even deserve to be called theologians).

A point common to this wide range of authors, however, is that of practically never referring to the principle of authority as proof in favour of the need to keep the substance of the Nicene-Constantinopolitan Creed unchanged. This is not a question of indicating to simple people the contents to which it is necessary to adhere in order to preserve the faith of the Church intact in the midst of the alleged "crisis"; rather, it is intended to give readers the intellectual tools to react and counter-argue based on the same principles of post-conciliar theology and spirituality. Often the theses of the articles are supported by evidence of a philological, exegetical, historical nature (although, of course, always oriented by a general theological vision); contemporary philosophers and sociologists are happily cited[12]; the plausibility of some doctrines is sometimes supported by arguments of an existential nature. Precisely because they were aware of taking up defensive positions, the *Communio* theologians did everything they could to avoid being accused of conservatism; sometimes it even seems that they are careful to make their criticisms of progressive theology sound like a sort of "overreach from the left". For example, Bouyer (and elsewhere de Lubac) discredits the nascent contemporary theological movement by denouncing its similarities with pre-conciliar neo-scholasticism: for the despotic attitude, for the scientific and non-confessional approach to theology, for the way in which it develops themes such as the theology of grace[13].

Furthermore, there is often an appeal to the "ethical proof" guaranteed by great figures of twentieth-century theological renewal, such as Karl Barth and Teilhard de Chardin, quotations from whom are used to support the authors' opinions. From this perspective (and perhaps in implicit controversy with the rival Concilium, more masculine and clerical?), we can also read the fact that, especially in France, the journal lays claim to the strong lay and female component of the team[14].

3. Conclusions

If to a large extent the Credo of Paul VI and the articles of *Communio* have the same polemical objectives and give shape to the same concern for a "defence of the faith", the style is decidedly different. The former presents the faithful with content to be believed by force of the authority of tradition and the Petrine magisterium, the latter instead strives to carry forward an identity defence of the uniqueness of the Christian fact, and to justify in various ways the universal normative nature of "integral Catholicism"[15].

Even the authors of *Communio*, however, do not consider in all their seriousness the difficulties and objections raised by the contemporary context relating to the maintenance of a dogmatic apparatus of beliefs. As we have seen in relation to the Creed, they did not enter into a real dialogue with the theologians who in that period seized the temptation of the times to try to return to the radical nature of the Gospel, but generally limited themselves to attacking them, disavowing them, and dismissing their attempts as so many betrayals of faith.

Under the banners of *Concilium* and *Communio*, in fact, a clash between different and incompatible, yet mirror-like theological paradigms would increasingly take shape: both journals claim in their own way the moral strength of the Council, both propose to confess a faith that is truly credible for humanity today, in the face of progress in science and philosophies. For the theologians of *Communio*, it was not a rearguard fight, motivated by the Roman desire to defend this or that article of the Catholic faith and founded on a rigid and neo-Thomistic conception of the Maritainian truth; at stake was the defence of the patristic *Logos* placed at the foundation of the universality and aal-embracing claim of the Christian phenomenon.

This principle, which had been brought back into fashion by the *nouvelle théologie*, would constitute one of the main features of the theological option with which the pontificate of John Paul II would become magisterium, and the heart of the identity project which would be implemented under the name of New Evangelisation[16]. It is no longer a question of pastors who combat some erroneous opinions (think of the ten errors cited in Ottaviani's letter in 1966, or of the various critical points evoked in the Credo of Paul VI), but of theologians who carry out a real "question of principle". Perhaps it is also for this reason that in the following decade, when it was managed by John Paul II and Cardinal Ratzinger as Prefect of the doctrinal Congregation, the controversy on the foundations of the faith became much more intransigent and violent.

Notes

1. Renato Papetti (ed.), La trasmissione della Fede: L'impegno di Paolo VI, Rome/Brescia: Istituto Paolo VI, 2009. See especially M. Cagin, "Le «Credo du Peuple de Dieu» et l'année de la foi," 157–179, here 170–173 in relation to the plan for a "kerygmatic Creed" which Congar had sent to Paul VI, with the request to pronouce it solemnly at the end of the Council. On that occasion the pope reportedly rejected the proposal; three years later, however, on the basis of the schema advanced by Maritain – very different in content from the first – he accepted.
2. Among the additions are the emphasis on an anti-subordinationist Christology, on Marian dogmas and the doctrine of transubstantiation. The text of the profession of faith pronounced by the pope is in Insegnamenti di Paolo VI, vol.: VI, Città del Vaticano: Tipografia Poliglotta Vaticana, 1968, 300–310.
3. In the very first edition, Henri de Lubac, "Credo... Sanctorum Communionem," Internationale katholische Zeitschrift: *Communio* (1/1972) 18–32; Cf. also Wolfgang Beinert, "Die alten Glaubensbekenntnisse und die neuen Kurzformeln, " Internationale katholische Zeitschrift: *Communio* (2/1972) 97–114 and Joseph Ratzinger, "Noch einmal: "Kurzformeln des Glaubens": Anmerkungen," Internationale katholische Zeitschrift. *Communio* (3/1973) 258–264.
4. Cf. Klaus Reinhardt, "In what way is Jesus Christ unique?," *Communio International Catholic Review* (Winter 1974) 343–364, here 360; see also the critique of the de-Hellenisation in Roch Kereszty, "Reflections on the foundations of Christology," 385–393.
5. The Italian edition is entitled "credo in un solo Dio". The first four articles common to the two versions are: Henri de Lubac, "Introduzione al Credo," Strumento internazionale per un lavoro teologico", *Communio* 19 (1975) 3–8; Joseph Ratzinger, "Credo in Dio Padre onnipotente," 9–14; Louis Massignon, "Le tre preghiere d'Abramo (1949)," 15–20; Ferdinand Ulrich, "Dio nostro padre," 32–38.
6. In relation to the topic in question here, the articles by Jean-Luc Marion, Jacques Guillet, Louis Bouyer and André Leonard are of particular importance. Note also the "place of honour" that the Creed held in the journal's presentation brochure released as early

as April 1975 – "Communio vise avant tout à confesser la foi catholique, c'est-à-dire indissolublement : formuler le Credo grâce à un langage assez rigoureux pour en exprimer la cohérence, les exigences et la puissance" – and the fact that, until 1980, every first issue of the year was dedicated to a reflection on a different Christological article of the Creed. Cf. Étienne Fouilloux, "Aux origines de *Communio* France (1969-1980)," in Bruno Dumons & Frédéric Gugelot (eds.), Catholicisme et identité: Regards croisés sur le catholicisme français contemporain (1980-2017), Paris: Karthala, 2017, 17–43, here 33 and 37 (to my knowledge, the contribution is the only historical study on *Communio* avaliable to date).

7   de Lubac, "Credo... Sanctorum Communionem," 32.
8   Cf. de Lubac, "Introduzione al Credo," 5: "Prima il rischio era dimenticare l'unità della fede a causa della molteplicità delle credenze, ora il rischio è l'opposto, cioè di non comprendere l'obbedienza della fede".
9   In various texts one can perceive a condemnation of the attempt that theology was making to encourage a dialogue on equal terms with the faithful of other religions; a model of religious pluralism is contrasted with the universalist inclusivism of a patristic approach (the issue is explcitly addressed by Kereszty, "Reflections on the foundations of Christology," 393). Especially from the 1990s the theme would become one of the main *Leitmotivs* of the journal.
10 Cf. Beinert, "Die alten Glaubensbekenntnisse," 106 and Ratzinger, "Kurzformeln des Glaubens," 261. In the article (on page 263) the philosophical proselytism practiced within Hellenistic Judaism to present the faith of Israel to the Greeks is also cited as a positive model; the reference to the Greek philosophical approach adopted by the Jewish world even before Christianity was one of the arguments that Ratzinger would most often put forward against de-Hellenisation.
11 J. Ratzinger, "Credo in Dio", 12.
12 Especially in reference to an epistemology in some ways already defined as post-modern: cf. Ratzinger, Io credo in Dio, and other contributions in this sense in subsequent issues, in which it will be argued that it is contemporary scientific reason itself that undermines the assumptions of modern reason.
13 Cf. L. Bouyer, "Situation de la théologie", Revue catholique internationale: *Communio* 1 (1975) 41–48: "Commençons donc par désamorcer ces deux sophismes : celui d'hier et celui d'aujourd'hui, dont il est bien caractéristique d'observer que c'est encore le premier qui survit derrière le second, à une inversion près" (42).
14 Cf. Fouilloux, "Aux origines de *Communio*," 42.
15 Cf. Fouilloux, "Aux origines de *Communio*," 33 and the experimental article by von Balthasar.
16 In July 1978, two months before Wojtyła became pope, Communio published an extract of the spiritual exercises he preached to the Roman Curia in 1976, on the Church's vocation to be a "sign of contradiction" before the "idols of modernity" (Giovanni Miccoli, In difesa della fede. La Chiesa di Giovanni Paolo II e Benedetto XVI, prima edizione, Milan: Rizzoli, 2007, p. 165 and Fouilloux, "Aux origines de Communio," 42).

Beyond the Filioque Controversy and the Symbols of Faith: The Rise of Pentecostal, Charismatic and Non-Denominational Christianity

VALENTINA CICILIOT

This article aims to look at the relationship between Pentecostal, charismatic and non-denominational Christianity and the Nicaean creed. Moving beyond the prejudicial assumption that the emergence on a global scale of these new forms of Christianity has obscured the centrality of the symbols of faith in contemporary Christian identity, it shows on one side the historical importance of the creed within classical Pentecostalism, particularly in the Jesus only/Oneness controversy, and on the other side the unnecessary character that this symbol represents for non-denominational bodies.

The prejudicial assumption behind the relationship between more recent forms of Christianity and the symbol of Nicaea is that the emergence and the spread on a global scale of Pentecostal-like and non-denominational churches have in some respects obscured the centrality of the symbols of faith in contemporary Christian identity, given the dogmatism with which these symbols have been clothed in the pneumatological discourse. As to say, the genetics of this new and global Christianity have not only lost the need to formulate theologically, once and for all, the essential of the Christian beliefs, rejecting more generally the systematization of the faith into theological formulas, but also have been anchored not to doctrinal elements such as creeds, but rather to the experiential sphere of faith. This paper aims to look at Pentecostal, charismatic, and non-denominational movements in order to find traces of the re-interpretation of the symbols of faith, particularly that of Nicaea-Constantinople, constructively articulating this relationship.

1. Definitions

Firstly, but briefly, it is necessary to define the object of this survey. *The New International Dictionary of Pentecostal and Charismatic Movements* traditionally identifies as "Pentecostal" the so-called classical Pentecostals connected with the U.S. revival at the Azusa Street Mission in Los Angeles (1906-1909); the members of the so-called charismatic movements in the established Roman Catholic, Protestant, and Orthodox churches that surfaced in North America during the 1960s;[1] and the so-called neo-charismatic groups, "a catch-all category that comprises independent, indigenous, post-denominational – sometimes synonymous of non-denominational – denominations and groups that cannot be classified as either Pentecostal or charismatic but share a common emphasis on the Holy Spirit, spiritual gifts, Pentecostal-like experiences (not Pentecostal terminology), signs and wonders, and power encounters", putting together neo-charismatics and non-denominational entities.[2] However, the use of the term "Pentecostal" as a broad and inclusive category for describing globally movements and denominations that emphasize the gifts of the Spirit, both on phenomenological and on theological perspectives, has been used since the beginning of the 2000s – Allan Anderson, for example, is intended to emphasize multicentric Pentecostalism's cultural diversity and includes classical Pentecostal, charismatic, and neo-Pentecostal/neo-charismatic groups, also in an attempt to decentralize the North American origins of these phenomena.[3] Another option has been proposed: the use of the term "Pentecostalisms" in the plural, instead of the singular, partially related to the attempt mentioned before. For example, the choice of this terminology by Cecil M. Robeck, Jr. comes in response to the North American tendency to interpret Pentecostalism mono-culturally from the perspective of American cultural history with little or no reference to the legitimate cultural divergence of Pentecostal faith and practice in other countries around the world.[4] But the plural designation has been also used to emphasize not only the sociocultural locations of these communities but also the differences in doctrine, liturgy, politics, or church government.[5] Whatever terminology one wants to use, Pentecostals, charismatics, and neo-charismatics are linked together and often handled as interchangeable terms.

2. Pentecostal/Charismatic/Non-Denominational Christianity and the Symbols of Faith

It is safe to say that, in the absence of central authority, these types of Christians have evolved into a diverse theological tradition throughout their history, mostly under the influence of denominational leaders or popular preachers. On a general level, although Pentecostal and charismatic denominations have not officially adopted the historic creeds as statements of faith, they don't reject these symbols. As Keith Warrington writes, Pentecostals have "(often unknowingly) affirmed the classical creeds, adopting the orthodox beliefs of the Western Church, as defined by the Council of Nicaea."[6] There are also a few cases in which the official creeds are explicitly mentioned such as for the International Pentecostal Holiness Church (IPHC) – which claims to have 1,500,000 members and over 1,600 congregations in the United States, Methodist episcopal heritage –, which identifies its "roots in historic Christianity as we affirm the Apostles' Creed, the Nicene Creed, and the Definition at Chalcedon." It also affirms that:

> Three streams of historic Christianity make up the theological and ecclesiastical foundations of the IPHC: 1. While we rejoice at the work of the Holy Spirit through church history, the IPHC was birthed in the theological heritage of the Protestant Reformation and the emphasis of Martin Luther on justification by faith alone, the supremacy of Scripture, and the priesthood of all believers. 2. We are also influenced by the holiness emphasis of the Anglican priest John Wesley. Our theological framework reflects Wesleyan holiness and Wesley's understanding of the Thirty-nine Articles of the Church of England. 3. Following the Azusa Street Revival in Los Angeles, California, in 1906, the message spread around the world of the Pentecostal baptism with the Holy Spirit. This dynamic understanding of Acts 2 and all the gifts of the Spirit being

available for the church today was received by the church and has characterized our life of worship of God, mission to the world, service to others, and fellowship with Christ's church.[7]

The first two above-mentioned historical traditions have in fact expressed the alignment with the traditional Christian creeds.

As you can read in one of the few online blogs on the relationship between Pentecostals and the creeds, the nowadays scenario is as follows:

Many people in Pentecostal churches have never heard the Creed, and some are even suspicious of it. The Creed, some people think, sounds like something Catholic, and so maybe a bit suspect. Or, others think, it sounds old-fashioned and irrelevant for a contemporary missional movement, and so maybe don't give it a second thought. Yet, although that may be how some people think about the Creed, that's probably got much more to do with the fact that the Creed is rarely mentioned or known among large sectors of Pentecostalism, than to do with any particularly Pentecostal attitude to the Creed (November 21, 2017).[8]

The irrelevance of the creeds for Pentecostals and the involvement of an anti-Catholic prejudice have, of course, historical reasons that have been synthesized here. Gerald T. Sheppard shows that movements of pneumatic enthusiasm such as those associated with Pentecostal and charismatic groups are "predicated on only a few points of doctrinal agreement, putting more emphasis on an ecumenicity inherent in the common experience of lives realized and secured in the power of the Holy Spirit."[9] Pentecostals usually regarded creeds as signs of "formalism", and denominationalism, preferring emphasizing the testimony. According to this perspective, creeds indicated a departure from apostolic faith for two reasons: 1. because of their lack of concern with practical Christianity, emphasizing formal doctrine instead; 2. because of their origin in and support for an episcopacy alien to the priesthood of believers, distancing them from the communitarian intimacy of the apostolic period.[10] The best example of this formalism and denominationalism or, better, creedalism, has been identified with the Catholic Church. Particularly at the beginning of classical Pentecostalism, objections to the Nicene creed have grown out of a yearning for "apostolic order" and the desire for a unified Christianity: in fact, there was a distinct disdain for creedalism within early Pentecostalism in an effort to avoid divisiveness and doctrinal disputes.[11] Pentecostal pioneers boasted in having "no creeds, rituals, or articles of faith" and "no creed but Christ or the Bible." So, the Nicene creed has been associated with the hierarchical apostolic succession and the episcopate of priests (vs the priesthood of all believers). Very few Pentecostals have voiced concrete doctrinal grounds for their rejection beyond concerns about the institutionalization of church structure and the formalization of doctrine at the cost of practical ministry.

A fundamental concern among early Pentecostals was not the doctrine or wording of the creed but its ecclesiological significance. Creeds were seen as destructive to the life of the church and synonymous with "isms" and "schisms" among communities.[12] As scholar Wolfgang Vonday puts it:

> Replacing God's law of unity with 'men-made creeds,' the Council of Nicaea was made primarily responsible for the initial disruption of the Christian fellowship. The challenge to adhere to the creedal proclamation of faith confronted first-generation classical Pentecostals with the ecumenical ecclesiology that was fundamental to their own movement. Pentecostals saw the creeds as ecumenical fences, a 'test of' in opposition to the unity of the separating the faithful from one another. In this sense, it did not matter whether the creedal statements were true or false, since they broke the law of love and unity. This separation was often experienced among Pentecostals in the harsh reality of persecution at the hands of the established churches. Ecclesiological and ecumenical concerns governed much of the Pentecostal hostility toward the adherence to creedal formulations.[13]

To a certain extent, it is safe to say that original ecumenism or better, that original Pentecostal ecumenicity have forced Pentecostals to diminish, if not obscure, the potentiality of the creeds, however, without opposing creeds in principle, but only under certain historical and geographical circumstances.

3. Oneness Pentecostalism, Trinitarian Pentecostalism and the Ecumenical Dialogue

The most famous example of such an opposition is the birth of Oneness Pentecostalism/Jesus Only Pentecostalism and the rise of the so-called "new issue" in 1913-1914, which illustrate the crisis of the creed in the twentieth century (estimated to have from 14 to over 17 million followers globally and growing rapidly in Mexico, China, and the United States). To sum up the "Jesus Only" Pentecostals argued the idea of the Trinity had been forced upon the church at Nicaea by the bishop of Rome and their criticism of Trinitarian theology began to push the Pentecostal understanding of apostolic faith more deeply into creedal issues. The issue was not only the Godhead but also the nature of Jesus Christ (they moved towards one God, a singular divine spirit with no distinction of persons who manifests himself in many ways, including as Father, Son, and Holy Spirit). The Oneness came to see the Nicene creed as a pagan document supportive of a trinitarian doctrine that was out of step with biblical revelation.

The "new issue" arose from the liturgical context of classical Pentecostalism and led to a division of Pentecostals into Oneness and Trinitarian camps.[14] According to Vonday, the emphasis on the liturgical origins of the debate is important on at least two levels. First, the debate emerged amidst the widely attended camp meetings that shaped the early Pentecostal liturgy and the cultural and ecclesiastical diversity of classical Pentecostalism. Second, it emerged in the explicit context of the administration of water baptism, the understanding of the baptismal mode, and the question of the correct baptismal formula, mirroring the liturgical seedbed of the creeds. The consequences of this debate did not immediately emerge as Trinitarian questions but unfolded on the basis of a distinction in liturgical praxis between the single name of Jesus and the three titles "Father," "Son," and "Holy Spirit." In this context, the triadic structure of the creed emerged as a dividing line between adherents of the Oneness and Trinitarian Pentecostal positions. So, the Council of Nicaea emerges here as a watershed between the Oneness and Trinitarian views of God, showing the historical importance of that creed also among Pentecostals.[15]

If the above-mentioned ecumenicity has been a key element for the indifference/obscuration towards the creeds, the contemporary ecumenical dialogue with the other Christian confessions has demanded classical Pentecostals to reopen the debate on the creeds. As a matter of fact, the Nicene creed and the subsequent development of Trinitarian orthodoxy have been regarded by many as essential to the apostolic faith of the churches. For example, the Nicene-Constantinopolitan creed without the filioque clause was made the starting point of the World Council of Churches' Commission on Faith and Order study program entitled *Towards the Common Expression of the Apostolic Faith Today*, initiated in Lima 1982. In this context, the divisions of oneness and trinitarian Pentecostals represent a problematic issue, even if these two groups have entered a dialogue in the late 1990s thanks to the Society for Pentecostal Studies.[16] After all, Vonday argues that "the crisis of global Christianity is also a crisis of its creedal tradition" since the creeds have been the "single most dividing issue, and the most dominant and persistent problem of theological discourse"[17]: for the West because of the addition of the filioque clause to the Nicene-Constantinopolitan creed and for the Pentecostals because of the internal division on trinitarian aspects.

4. Megachurches and Nicaea

Moving from Pentecostals to more recent neo-charismatics and non-denominational groups, more nuances can be seen (and here the term "non-denominational" is used to identify subjects that do not affiliate with any established denomination or mainstream/historical church that often separate themselves from the strict doctrine and customs of other Christian fellowships, typically distancing themselves from confessionalism and creedalism). These new entities are more revolutionary in form – style, cult, and organizational structure (also the places they occupy, such as airports, and malls) – than in content (they tend not to present new theological trends or new doctrines). Centralized and hierarchical organizational structures, typical of historical churches have been replaced by a looser and more local dimension, focused on the needs of believers. Their main characteristics are as follows: seminary training of clergy is optional and lay leadership is highly valued; worship is simple, non-liturgical, providing an opportunity for people to access the sacred in a personal way, it is bodily, rather than merely cognitive, valuing religious experience; they tend to have extensive small-group ministries, focusing on intimacy and avoidance of bureaucracy; the gifts of the Holy Spirit are central; Bible-centered teaching predominate over topical sermonizing, expressing doctrinal minimalism.[18] Logically all these features result in an indifference to the historical symbols of faith. If one looks at the biggest megachurches in the world – defined as a church with a sustained average attendance of at least 2,000 per week that often sociologists have used concerning non-denominational groups –, they completely ignore any doctrinal debate on the creeds: the website and related online platforms of the major non-denominational megachurches, such as Calvary Temple and New Life Fellowship in India, Lakewood Church and Church of the Highlands in the US, or Christ Commission Fellowship in the Philippines have shown no mentions of the symbols of faith.[19] Those bodies are not against the historical symbols such as that of Nicaea, but simply those are not formulas through which they express their faith. They often offer to believers their "statements of faith" – mostly expressing trinitarianism –, but they prefer to justify them with the use of biblical passages rather than conciliar documents or historical ecclesiastical proclamations. It is possible that, if these congregations ever enter the ecumenical dialogue with the historic churches, a Pentecostal-like attitude will be triggered, and the creeds will become less marginalized…

5. Conclusion

In conclusion, this contribution demonstrates how the symbols of faith, although practically unnecessary, when not initially rejected, in the rise of Pentecostal and charismatic Christianity, have played a non-secondary role within classical Pentecostalism and are playing a role in the contemporary ecumenical dialogue between Pentecostals/charismatics and the historical/mainline churches. Non-denominational bodies do not ban the Nicaean creed, but it is simply absent from their statements of faith. This article also demonstrates how this creed has shown a capacity for adaptation within global Christianity: in spite of any thesis that tends to crystallize it in rigid and perpetual theological formulas, it has actually been a dynamic expression of the Christian faith, charged with universal value but at the same time open to processes of enculturation.

Notes

1. Stanley M. Burgess, Eduard M. van der Maas (eds.), The New International Dictionary of Pentecostal and Charismatic Movements, Grand Rapids, MI: Zondervan, 2002, Introduction, XVIII–XIX.
2. S. M. Burgess/E. M. van der Maas (eds.), The New International Dictionary of Pentecostal and Charismatic Movements, XX. Here there is the echo of the well-known sociological classification of the three "waves" of the Spirit: 1. Classical Pentecostalism, at the beginning of the XX century; 2. The charismatic movements within historical churches, in the 1960s; 3. The neo-charismatics, meaning the charismatics within US evangelicalism, in the 1980s.
3. Allan Anderson, An Introduction to Pentecostalism: Global Charismatic Christianity, Cambridge: Cambridge University Press, 2004, 13–14; Allan Anderson, "Diversity in the Definition of 'Pentecostal/Charismatic' and Its Ecumenical Implications," Mission Studies 19.1/2 (2002), 40–55.
4. Cecil M. Robeck, Jr., "Taking Stock of Pentecostalism: The Personal Reflections of a Retiring Editor," Pneuma 15.3 (1993), 35–60.
5. See Peter Beyer, Religions in Global Society, London: Routledge, 2006, 147–150; Daniel Chiquete, "Latin American Pentecostalism and Western Postmodernism: Reflections on a Complex Relationship," Internation Review of Mission 92.364 (2003), 29–39.
6. Keith Warrington, Pentecostal Theology Pentecostal Theology: A Theology of Encounter, London/New York: T.&T. Clark, 2008, 29.
7. https://iphc.org/introduction/. Last access 30/06/2024.
8. https://www.apostolictheology.org/2017/11/pentecostals-and-creed.html led by Jonathan Black, a pastor and teacher in the Apostolic Church in the UK. (out of the Welsh revival, 1904-1905). See also https://www.youtube.com/watch?v=fS7fHcS3i2E&ab_channel=JonathanBlack. Last access 30/06/2024.
9. See Gerald T. Sheppard, "The Nicean Creed, Filioque, and Pentecostal Movements in the United States," Greek Orthodox Theological Review 31.3-4 (1986), 401–416, here 172.
10. G. T. Sheppard, "The Nicean Creed," 405.
11. Frank D. Macchia, "The Oneness-Trinitarian Pentecostal Dialogue: Exploring the Diversity of Apostolic Faith," The Harvard Theological Review, 103.3 (2010), 329–349.
12. Wolfgang Vonday, Beyond Pentecostalism: The Crisis of Global Christianity and the Renewal of the Theological Agenda, Grand Rapids, MI/Cambridge, UK: Eerdmans, chapter 3 (epub version).
13. Vonday, Beyond Pentecostalism, 175.
14. F. D. Macchia, "The Oneness-Trinitarian Pentecostal Dialogue," 335–340.
15. Vonday, Beyond Pentecostalism, 176–183.
16. "Oneness-Trinitarian Pentecostal Final Report," Pneuma 30 (2008), 203–224.
17. Vonday, Beyond Pentecostalism, 157–158
18. See the classical Donald E. Miller, "Postdenomnational Christianity in the Twenty-First Century," The Annals of the American Academy of Political and Social Science 558 (Jul.1998), 196–210.
19. See the following websites as examples: https://calvarytemple.in/About-us; https://nlfa.org/church.html#about; https://www.lakewoodchurch.com/about; https://www.churchofthehighlands.com/about; https://www.ccf.org.ph/who-we-are/.

Contributions from feminist theology to trinitarian theology. Reimagining the notion of "relationality"

SILVIA MARTÍNEZ CANO

Feminist theologies offer a renewed language which re-signifies the principal metaphors linked to the trinitarian God. They approach the subject from the perspective of gender, integrating this with other categories of analysis used to examine trinitarian theology (ethnicity, geography, class etc.). This enables an epistemological, hermeneutic, and pastoral advancement, which improves the connection between reflection on the Trinity and trinitarian practice in the Christian community. In this text, we explore the work of various authors whose writing on the subject of trinitarian models has been conceived with an emphasis on creative fidelity, diversity of models, and pastoral concern.

1. To name God: to return to the heart of the trinitarian symbol

The doctrine of the Trinity has experienced a complex and contested theological development within the central corpus of Christianity. Its traditional formulation, being dependent on classical metaphysics, makes it difficult to express and to understand. These conditions have meant that over the course of history, the communal experience of God the Trinity has become distanced from the abstract speculations of theologians. After the Vatican II council there was a marked renewal of interest in the subject, and theologians experimented with new approaches to it. Feminist theology which, from its beginnings in the 50s and 60s of the twentieth century, had focused on critiquing patriarchal theological language, saw this moment as an opportunity to offer a renewed form of language which re-signified the principle metaphors linked to the trinitarian God.

This reimagining of the analogue and metaphoric language surrounding "Naming God" was done collegiately, that is to say, that it attempted to address the diversity of distinct contexts which those who wrote on the subject came from, and the perspectives related to gender which they brought with them, alongside other categories of theological analysis (ethnicity, geography, class etc.). It is necessary therefore, to talk of a plurality of focuses, epistemologies, hermeneutics, systematic formulations, and pastoral applications. What these feminist theologians sought was an epistemological advance towards an understanding the special relationship between God and his creation – one characterised by freedom and salvation – through intersectional hermeneutic categories, which contributes to theological thinking on relationships, while leaving behind a dualistic understanding of reality (transcendent-immanent, body-soul, efficiency-gratuity)[1].

In many cases, feminist theologians opted to analyse the heart of the trinitarian symbol, returning to the original formulations of Nicaea and to the context from which it emerged. With these insights they evaluated the possibility of a similar project of contemporary inculturation. In general, they agreed that Nicaea made it necessary to examine the source of metaphysics in order to refine its definition. Their debates were more Christological than trinitarian, for in play was the articulation of the double nature of Jesus Christ. As its semantics were built, the dogma remained Hellenised and lost its dynamic and relational character. As a result, it strayed from its other objective – to serve as a regulatory structure for comprehending the Symbol. Paradoxically, its definition, which sought to avoid a hierarchical understanding of divinity, ended up reinforcing it. Furthermore, it was converted into a useful tool for detecting heretics and an obstacle to helping the faithful to live their faith[2].

The deal was finally synthesised by scholasticism, especially by Thomas Aquinas and Buenaventura de Fidanza. The second scholasticism and the theological schools of the counter-reformation engaged in successive reformulations of trinitarian ministry, and this resulted in the disconnection of the symbol from its practical character; leading, in its philosophical abstraction, to deistic, theistic, agnostic, and even atheistic positions.

Being conscious of this situation, the majority of feminist theologians reaffirmed that it is the very doctrine of the Trinity which saves theology from suffocating androcentrism. Firstly, because it preserved the alterity of God, that is to say, it mitigates the threat of androcentrism which drowns the experience of gratitude and divine sacrifice. In this way it defeats the conception of a solitary, indifferent, and monarchical God – a frequent feature of feminist critiques.

Secondly, because the trinitarian God is not masculine, despite multiple, majoritarian, and unsatisfactory anthropomorphic representations – fruit of patriarchal and hierarchical structures in which Christianity has been housed, and which apply their androcentric social models to the image of God. It is unfortunate that God is incarnated in masculine form, the gendered and limited condition of the incarnation being the key revelation of the logic of divine love. God, in his infinite love and manifested in Jesus Christ, is perceived to be incarnated within the historical-temporal limits of this culture. Jesus, the man, possesses an alternative and transgressive masculinity which enables a rethinking of what it is to be human beyond his gendered reality.

Thirdly, the baptismal formula which formed part of the first Christian community (for example, see 1 Corinthians 1: 4-5; Matthew 28: 18-20; or Acts 2: 38) contains its own self-subversion: we are baptised "in the name" (singular) of God, the Son, and the Holy Spirit", and not "in the names" (plural) of two or three men. The words "Father" and "Son" in the formulas are not biological or hierarchical roles of power, but expressions of the relationship of love and sacrifice.

Fourthly, the trinitarian formulation respects, reinforces, and supports a caring vision of God, which gives a constant and clear form to the person of Jesus Christ, and reminds believers of the path to the fulfilment of creation.

Finally, some feminist theologies point out that the voices of the 20th century which affirm that trinitarian doctrine has exhausted its usefulness in a new cultural context demonstrate that trinitarian doctrine is always a challenge. They provide a reminder that patriarchal binarism – in the fact that you can only have one or the other, the superior or the inferior, the masculine or the feminine – means that God the Trinity is always in question. Furthermore, they exhort us to study the efforts of the first churches to inculturate the new language of a plural and globalised era.

Faithful to this exhortation, feminist theologians who have delved into the trinitarian treatise have endeavoured to propose semantic alternatives, with a vocabulary which draws from other scientific disciplines developed in the past century – phenomenology, anthropology, sociology, psychology, pedagogy, aesthetics, and the renovated philosophy which emerged at the end of the century. The alternatives are oriented towards improving comprehension of the theological notion of "relationality" – something which is central to the trinitarian symbol. Furthermore, they take three key epistemologies into account: creative fidelity, diversity of models, and pastoral concern.

2. The Necessity of dialoguing with tradition. Creative fidelity

While not everyone is in agreement, many of these theologians admit that the solution is not a total rejection of the Hellenised doctrine of the Trinity, but that it is instead possible to create a continuation of the tradition through a de-Hellenised form of language, without being obligated to utilise de-situated and patriarchal terminology. Rejecting the tradition completely could provoke a breach in the transmission of faith which would produce a profound trauma within the Christian community[3]. At the same time, they warn that not inculcating this language, and offering only one masculinised way of understanding the Trinity, has already created a gap which is sufficiently painful and difficult to bridge that it hurts the church. Because of this, the way to connect theology to contemporary life is through negotiation with traditional theological language.

This requires three processes: 1) an initial deconstructive effort aimed at Hellenised semantics, to recuperate the original feelings and metaphors within their context; 2) an analysis of the meanings and their translation to our cultural world through the tension between what is said and not said, and the tension between experience and tradition; 3) a reconstruction of meanings, incorporating their own semantics with the globalised pluralism and de-colonialism within which we live, and which would produce a place for diverse, interdependent, and inclusive trinitarian models.

To activate these processes, some have dialogued with patriarchal tradition, especially with the Cappadocian fathers of the fourth century, thus recovering their fluid dialectics between the resources of reason (cataphatic theology) and the recognition of the ineffable transcendence of the Mystery (apophatic theology), where only silence and metaphorical language fit. They have also dialogued with classic scholasticism (especially with Saint Thomas) from a critical position and with a gender-based perspective to both rethink concepts and develop new ones, while turning to biblical sources to recover the diverse nuances of the plurality of the names of God (Catherine M. LaCugna[4] and Elisabeth A. Johnson[5]). Other theologians have proposed stable models which make it possible to understand trinitarian dynamism by incorporating a new vocabulary to widen the paths which drive the trinitarian experience (Sallie McFague[6] and Janet M. Soskice[7] among others[8]).

They also note that negotiation with, and the continuity of, the Trinitarian doctrine cannot be obtained through a new but fixed formulation, resistant to all critique. On the contrary, negotiation and its processes serves as a framework for a hermeneutic which accepts the uncertainty of contemporary challenges. By analysing and deconstructing the oppressive and patriarchal elements which cloud our view of the God of dynamic Love[9], it is possible to continue affirming that God is love in the face of scientific and social idolatry, individual and hedonistic consumerism (science, truth, money, consumption, success, security, possession, power, violence), and all the idolatries at the service of domination and oppression.

3. The necessity of new models

The second key hermeneutic is to recuperate the potential of narrative language, rendered more appropriate for our time, in order to provide diversity to monarchical trinitarian models and to the communion. Theologians such as LaCugna propose distinct metaphorical models of God, with a wider and more diverse narrative which can be better heard and understood by the community[10].

McFague argues that metaphoric theology recuperates the apophatic character of the metaphor itself through a dynamic equilibrium between speculation and imagination. It is not possible to escape the conflict between interpretations, just as it is not possible to escape the injustice of life (hunger, suffering, violence), and this makes theology a concrete action, committed to the creaturely condition of all creation. To welcome, to deny, and to transform are the tasks of theology. Through this dynamic, theology locates the places of rupture with Hellenised doctrine, and proposes concepts and hypotheses through stable metaphors or models that build new bridges for trinitarian theology.

Soskice argues that models and metaphors, while distinct and not directly comparable categories – despite frequently being treated as such by patriarchal theology – are intimately linked[11]: both remind us of the elusive character of God while highlighting the diversity of nuances of what they narrate, maintaining contact with the imaginaries of culture, whether through art or visual culture, ecological sensitivity, the virtual imaginary or other types of imaginaries. These models are great fields of metaphor, associated with visual representations such as abstract concepts, emotions, feelings, senses or judgements. The act of utilising visual and narrative images of God puts us in symphony with the narrative language of the present day, and flexibly accepts the locability of human beings, as well as the contributions that each culture contributes to discussions about God within its own context. Some metaphors are already present in Christian tradition, for example the classic metaphor of the sun (God), his rays (the Son) and his heat (the Holy Spirit) which Gregory of Nazianzus transformed into the image of three suns emitting a single ray[12]. Through them, it is possible to generate new metaphors of colours, digital elements or virtual transformations.

Some examples of the models proposed by feminist theologians reevaluate biblical images and meanings to make them resonate with believer's experiences today. For example, faced with the immutable essence of God, Soskice suggests recreating images linked to the metaphorical field of mercy (*rahamin*) and to the tender feelings of God towards creation. God is revealed as a God possessing maternal organs, who empathises with those who suffer and is not indifferent. From the prophetic tradition (Hosea 11: 1-9; Isaiah 49: 15; Jeremiah 31: 20; Deuteronomy 32: 10) God reveals through the incarnation (Philippians 2: 6-8) that salvation is drawn from weakness and impotence: from death to life, from hostility to solidarity, and from pain to joy.

Johnson attempts to recover the biblical tradition of Wisdom (hokmah), a feminine reference which she presents as being comprised of the presence or secondary name of God (Proverbs 8: 22-31). Wisdom is found in the manifestation of God; it is the strength born from the presence of God which penetrates everything. Intimately connected to prudence, intelligence, valour and justice, wisdom breathes life into creation

(Proverbs 8: 35). This is how Johnson articulates the trinitarian symbol while avoiding masculinised terminology: Shekinah (presence), Hokmah-Dabar (wisdom-word) and Ruah (Holy Spirit).

For her part, McFague articulates the Trinitarian symbol through the category of *ágape*, because in selfless love, bonds of friendship between people arise: as a free relation, but at the same time creating a connection. In this way liberty, confidence and friendship are the fundamental experiences which define the meeting with God through free communication. McFague names the three most intimate models of relationship which represent the creative, salvatory, and sustaining activity of God in relation to the world: the Mother God (creator, protector, and provider of life's nutrition), Lover (saviour, cleaner, and loyal), and Friend (sustainer of relationships).

In this way, other theologians have strengthened the Holy Spirit's role as a protagonist as well as its feminist biblical roots, in order to establish the trinitarian dynamic. For example, Sarah Coackley defends those who emphasise the links between the Holy Spirit and trinitarian reflection through the practice of oration and the cult, thus defusing the misleading idea that the problem of the Trinity can be "solved" by rational thought. At the same time, she warns against the new risk of creating "sentimental" versions of feminine images of God, which perpetuate stereotypes and once again feed patriarchal orthodoxy[13].

On the other hand, some proposals reimagine the trinitarian essence through new language. The starting point for them, is the tradition itself[14]. Some ideas, present in this tradition, incorporate the elements of our own time or re-signify concepts using today's meanings.

For example, LaCugna considers that the contributions to the formulation of the doctrine of the Trinity, made after Nicaea by the fathers of Cappadocia (Basil of Caesarea, Gregory of Nyssa and Gregory of Nazianzus), put excessive emphasis on the incomprehensible and unnameable essence of God. The use of the term "person" as a relational term by the Capadocians can resonate with the communicative sensibilities of today, however. People – as much human as divine – are essentially relational and not autonomous. In the same manner, people – while distinct and unique – should never be considered subordinate to others. Here, a relationship of interdependence between the human being and God is drawn, fully expressed in the perichoresis of the Trinity[15].

For many authors (Johnson, LaCugna, Greshake, Soskice) the perichoretic element is understood as a "dance around"[16]. The Trinity is love in movement, that is to say, a community which dances. The immanent trinitarian God is neither situated inside reality or against it, but instead is always loyal to it and in its favour. This is a passionate God which, in the joyful game of the dance, from its intimate relationality and its infinite wisdom, liberates, cleanses, and strengthens creation. The divine life is a perichoretic effusion of love, and a loving interdependence[17].

Another contribution is the re-dimensioning of the experience of God as Creator-Saviour and as Redeemer-Sustainer. The first model refers to the nutritional relationship: "all that is" is liberally created and its existence is continually maintained by God. There is therefore, a necessary and loving relationship between God and creation which is expressed in terms of *sustenance*. Creation, and within it the human being, is shown to be connected to a God who is deeply involved with this creation. The trinitarian name of God equates to the divine promise to always provide nutrition for life. The second model goes further. McFague argues that the model of the world as "the body of God" (in the sense of a divine promise which always sustains) is more appropriate for our times than the model of creation as the Kingdom of God. Although these two models have risks when it comes to their interpretation – the first as a possible form of pantheism, and the second as an authoritarian and hierarchical deism – the ecological crisis invites us to understand that the relationship with God emerges from interior care rather than exterior intervention. Because of this, the concepts of vulnerability, shared responsibility, and risk must be present in reflections on the trinitarian God.

The consequence of this ecofeminist view of the relationship with God, is hermeneutic: the re-imagination of the human being as an *imago trinitatis*. The "God who dances" puts its efforts into the love of bodies which "are" in creation. It is in the encounter between bodies that divine mercy acts, expressing perichoretic love, cleansing and saving matter, and banishing the long-held idea within the Christian tradition that the corporeal is opposed to the spiritual. Salvation of the trinitarian God today comes through corporeal incarnation, revealed in the fullness of Jesus Christ which reconciles the corporeal with trinitarian life. This notion redimensions the formula of *imago dei*, and invites us to think as *imago trinitaris*, because we are bodies which participate in the dance of God, not in an immersive form, but through the encounter[18].

4. The pastoral concern. Conclusions

The encounter with the "God who dances" situates us within a trinitarian movement through which "we live, we move and we exist" (Acts 17: 28). This encounter occurs, not because of a specified use of its Greek categories, but because of its soteriological and historical implications for the daily life of the Christian community. Thus, the pastoral dimension of the Trinitarian treaty is a path which can be followed in the context of this century. A completely-relational God, through a reciprocal exchange of love, is implicated and committed to action in a world in conflict, which is in need of tenderness. God is action in solidarity, lovingly uniting us with him (filiation), making us siblings of Jesus (fraternity-sorority), and leading us to encounter the body of God (communion-circularity)[19].

Because of this (and returning to our initial dilemma), can the Trinitarian doctrine use this diversity of models to serve as a regulatory framework, as it did in the past? If the very nature of God involves being in relationship with (being-toward, being-for), then "Trinity" is the name of the force which is God-for-us. In this manner the immanent Trinity and the economic Trinity can be encountered: who God is (in Himself) is fully revealed through the economic activities of creating, redeeming-healing and sustaining (being towards), and these economic activities are constitutive of God's being (being itself). His ontology is expressed through the tenderness of the relational.

For this reason, today pastoral practice should be oriented toward thinking and living God as the "home of communion."[20], and the shared (or *agapic*) table which welcomes us, surprises us, commits us to it, and makes us a single and plural community of faith through him.

Translated by Max Serjeant

Notes

1 María Clara Bingemer, "La Trinidad a partir de la perspectiva de la mujer. Algunas pautas para la reflexión", in Elsa Támez (ed.), El Rostro femenino de la teología, Costa Rica: DEI 1986, 135–165, 137–139.

2 Cf. Janet Martin Soskice, "Trinity and feminism", in Susan Frank Parsons (ed.), The Cambridge Companion to Feminist Theology, Cambridge: Cambridge University Press, 2002, 135–150, 138.
3 Cf. Margaret D. Kamitsuka, Feminist Theology and the Challenge of Difference, New York: Oxford University Press, 2007, 117.
4 Cf. Catherine LaCugna, God for Us, San Franscisco, CA: Harper San Francisco, 1991; Catherine LaCugna, "God in Communion with Us", in C. LaCugna (ed.) Freeing Theology: The Essentials of Theology in Feminist Perspective, New York: Harper Collins, 1993.
5 Cf. Elizabeth A. Johnson, She Who Is. The Mystery of God in Feminist Theological Discourse, New York: Crossroad, 1992 [published in Spanish as: Elizabeth A. Johnson, La que es: El misterio de Dios en el discurso teológico feminista, Barcelona: Herder, 2002]
6 Cf. Sallie McFague, Models of God: Theology for an Ecological Nuclear Age, Fortress Press, 1987 [Published in Spanish as: Sallie McFague, Modelos de Dios. Teología para una era ecológica y nuclear, Santander: Sal Terrae, 2002]; Sallie McFague, Metaphorical Theology: Models of God in Religious Language, Philadelphia: Augsburg Fortress Publishers, 1982.
7 Cf. Janet Martin Soskice, The Kindness of God, Oxford: Oxford University Press, 2007; Janet Martin Soskice, "Trinity and 'the feminine Other'", New Blackfriars 75/878 (1994) 2–17; Janet Martin Soskice, "Can a Feminist Call God "Father"?", in Alvin Kimmel (ed.), The Holy Trinity and the Challenge of Feminism, New York: Eerdmans, 1992, 81–94.
8 For example, see: Mary Grey, "The Core of our Desire: Re-Imaging the Trinity", Theology 93 (1990), 363–72; Isabel Gómez Acebo (ed.) Así vemos a Dios, Bilbao: Desclée De Brouwer, 2001; Ivone Gebara, Longing for Running Water. Ecofeminsm and Liberation, Minneapolis: Fortress Press, 1999; Montserrat Escribano, Dios, deseo y subversion. La vida trinitaria de las mujeres, Estella: Verbo Divino, 2021.
9 Cf. Verna E. F. Harrison, "Male And Female in Cappadocian Theology", Journal of Theological Studies 41/2 (1990), 441–471; Verna E. F. Harrison, "Illuminated from All Sides by the Trinity: Neglected Themes in Gregory Nazianzens Trinitarian Theology", in Christopher A. Beeley (ed.), Re-Reading Gregory of Nazianzus: Essays on History, Theology, and Culture, New York: The Catholic University of America Press, 2012, 13–30.
10 Catherine Mowry LaCugna, "Re-Conception the Trinity as the Mystery of Salvation", Scottish Journal of Theology 38/1 (1985), 21.
11 Cf. Janet Martin Soskice, Metaphor And Religious Language, Oxford: Clarendon Press, 1985, 55.
12 Cf. Gregorio de Nacianzo, Los cinco discursos teológicos, Madrid: Ciudad Nueva, 1995, discurso 31(5), 261–265.
13 Cf. Sarah Coakley, God, Sexuality, and the Self: An Essay 'On The Trinity', Cambridge: Cambridge University Press, 2013, 101–110, aquí 104; Sarah Coakley, "'Feminity" and the Holy Spirit?' in Monica Furlong (ed.), Mirror to the Church, London, SPCK, 1988.
14 There are also divergences on this point. For example, Mary Daly undoes the language of tradition to create a new one (Mary Daly, Beyond God the Father. Towards a Philosophy of Women´s Liberation (Beacon Press: Boston, 1973); Mary Daly, Pura Lujuria. Filosofía Feminista fundamental (Cátedra: Madrid 2023) and Catherine LaCugna

apuesta por un lenguaje adaptado en diálogo con Agustín de Hipona y Tomás de Aquino (cf. LaCugna, God for Us…).

15 Perhaps the metaphors which impact us most today are personal ones involving an encounter, rather than the impersonal ones, such as the classic metaphors of Pseudodionysus of the channel-stream-river or root-trunk-branches. (cf. LaCugna, God for Us, 271–278)

16 Taken from Greek ("peri" meaning around and "choreo" meaning dance), and Latin ("circummincessio" meaning to advance around or to advance in an itinerary), (cf. Gisbert Greshake, Creer en el Dios uno y trino, Salamanca: Sígueme, 2002, 29); cf. LaCugna, God for Us, 272; Elizabeth A. Johnson, La que es, 38.

17 Cf. Soskice, Janet Martin, "Trinity and 'the Feminine Other'", New Blackfriars 75/878 (1994), 2–17. https://doi.org/10.1111/j.1741-2005.1994.tb01462.x; Soskice, The Kindness of God; Johnson, La que es…; LaCugna, God for Us; Cf. Sallie McFague, Modelos de Dios.

18 Cf. McFague, Modelos de Dios, 13.; Silvia Martínez-Cano, "Peregrinos de nosotros y nosotras mismas. Qué es el ser humano hoy", in García Maestro, Juan Pablo (comp.), ¿Qué cristianismo crea futuro?, Estella: Verbo Divino, 2023, 39–84.

19 Cf. Trinidad León, "El Dios relacional. El encuentro y la elusividad de un Dios comunicativo", in Isabel Gómez-Acebo (ed.), Así vemos a Dios, Bilbao: Desclée de Brouwer, 2001, 163–239, aquí 178; Socorro Vivas Albán, El Dios Trinidad: circularidad y encuentro in Elisa Estévez y Paula de Palma (eds.), Ventanas a la sinodalidad, Estella: Verbo Divino, (2023), 23–47, aquí 42–45.

20 Cf. Trinidad León Martín, "Experiencias de Dios en la vida cotidiana", Proyección 52 (2005) 159–173, aquí 163; Silvia Martínez-Cano, "La vida trinitaria de las mujeres. La subversión de la realidad", in Escribano, Trinidad, deseo y subversión, 183–216, aquí 206–208.

On the origins of the ecumenical re-appropriation of the Nicene faith (19th century)

LUCA FERRACCI

The Nicene-Constantinopolitan creed has returned to the centre of the ecumenical scene in view of the 2025 celebrations, without ever actually having left theological conversations: think of the last forty years of dialogue between the Catholic Church and the Orthodox Church, many of which were spent on the filioque question. It was re-discovered as the cornerstone of Christian unity by a theology that, in the nineteenth century, returned the fact of faith to the horizon of history and therefore relativised the doctrinal differences between the churches, allowing them to delve down again to the heart of the Christian faith. The road towards what would be one of the greatest conquests of the twentieth-century ecumenical movement was opened, among others, by the people and documents examined in this article: Johann A. Möhler, Ignaz von Döllinger and the Chicago-Lambeth Quadrilateral.

1. The urgency of an appointment

The almost frenetic activity of the churches and large ecumenical agencies in anticipation of 2025 seems to demonstrate how, after decades of sluggishness, the ecumenical movement is experiencing a sudden acceleration towards the horizon of those celebrations. Announced in September 2022 during the World Council of Churches' eleventh General Assembly in Karlsrühe, the sixth Faith and Order World Conference will take place in the Coptic monastery of Anba Bishoy in Wadi El-Natrun, near Alexandria, Egypt, in October 2025, thirty-two years after that of

Santiago de Compostela. With half-empty coffers and expectations reduced by a general and persistent ecclesial lethargy for the ecumenical cause, at least the theme of the conference seems to retain the spirit of the past: *Where Now for Visible Unity?*[1] And even though communion on the altar continues to be long in coming and the war in Eastern Europe shatters Orthodoxy in a mortar of blood and excommunications, after a century of appeals, curbs, and relaunches, the throne of Peter and the throne of Andrew hope that the time is ripe to meet in Nicaea and celebrate Easter together.

Far from deserving the blame of a low-intensity ecumenism that returns to the roots of faith because it is incapable of competing with the historical dynamism of the churches and doctrines, one hundred years of ecumenical passion for Nicaea and its creed – which is still a paltry proportion of the Christian era occupied by schisms – is in reality the tangible sign of the recovery of a "believing" dimension of catholicity, that is, of a universality which is no longer empirically measurable on the basis of ecclesial boundaries and defended by the weapons of apologetics, but believed and recognised in the symbol of faith and in the dynamic rhythm of history. Two moments of this slow ecumenical re-appropriation of Nicaea will be analysed below, both dating back to the nineteenth century, in which the Creed began to appear stripped of any theological-doctrinal superstructure and therefore was once again at stake in the destinies of the churches in search of unity.

2. The symbols, faith, history: Johann A. Möhler and Ignaz von Döllinger

Before returning to "the" creed, nineteenth-century theology returned to "creeds". Dominating this field is the figure of Johann Adam Möhler, herald of what is defined as the *Katholische Tübinger Schule* (Catholic Tübingen School), often identified with the faculty of Catholic Theology which had existed in the Swabian town since 1817.[2] The fame of this theologian, who began teaching as a full professor at Tübingen in 1828, when Catholics and Protestants had already been studying theology under the same roof for eleven years, is linked in fact to the *Symbolik*, a substantial comparative study of Catholic and Protestant teaching based on the professions of faith and the documents recognised as normative by the churches. The sense of this work, born in 1832 as a manual for students of the Catholic faculty, can be understood only through Möhler's journey and the development of his thought. In 1827, having until then devoted himself mainly to the study of the Church Fathers, gave a course on the theology of the creed and transcribed it with a view to publication. The same year, and the following year, he visited Germany's most renowned universities (Würzburg, Bamberg, Jena, Leipzig, Göttingen, and Berlin) where he met famous figures of Romanticism and also came into contact with the theology of *Erweckungsbewegung*, which in those years was bringing about the religious renewal of the German Protestant world. It was thanks to this experience that he distanced himself definitively from the Enlightenment rationalism he had absorbed in his formative years in order to embrace the idea of a living and community experience of faith. Hence the need to develop, in numerous drafts and five editions, a work which, while not expressly renouncing its apologetic and controversial intentions, was, as the author himself said in the first pages of his treatise, "a scientific exposition of the doctrinal differences among the various religious parties opposed to each other, in consequence of the ecclesiastical revolution of the sixteenth century, as these doctrinal differences are evidenced by the public confessions or symbolical books of those parties."[3]

It was this need to delve into the profound essence of the Christian message and to compare Catholic and Protestant dogmatics without apologetic malice that convinced a large part of twentieth-century theology, especially Catholic, of the fact that Möhler had found an entirely theological way to approach the problem of Christian unity. It was not a question of ascribing anachronistic ecumenical sensitivities to him, but of grasping all the implications of a theological thought that considered the doctrinal systems commensurable on the basis of their symbols of faith, and which therefore opened up to the possibility that Protestantism, despite its limits and its one-sidedness, was, for the Catholic Church a sort of "historical corrective", capable of infusing it by osmosis with that part of truth which had been neglected, distorted, or buried under centuries of disciplinary encrustations.

It was precisely that thinking historically about the deposit of faith, that respectful return to the sources, whereby experiences, revealed truths, and doctrinal fixations grow and adapt to continually evolving historical conditions, that fertilised so deeply so much of the terrain of subsequent theology, Catholic as well as Protestant. If traces of Möhler's dialectical conception of the development of dogmas, borrowed from Romantically-stamped Vitalism, can be found in a strand of Protestant theology that comes to Adolf von Harnack, the idea of the church as a material plurality guided by hierarchy and united by an interior vital principle, that is, the Holy Spirit, where the different partial propositions of the faith do not contradict each other, but rather complement each other, inspired in the Anglicanism of the late nineteenth century a conception of the inclusive and all-encompassing ecclesial unity that it had its pillars in the fundamental articles of the faith and in episcopal leadership in apostolic succession. On the Catholic side, however, it was the idea that Christianity had a historical status, rooted in the mystery of the incarnation itself, that bore the greatest fruit. The assumption that there existed a relationship between faith and history in which the Church, under the action of the Spirit, renews its awareness and preserves the memory of what it has received, has in fact proved crucial to the overcoming, in certain circles of Catholic theology, of the anti-historicism of neo-scholasticism and the doctrinal steadfastness with which the First Vatican Council had indicated to Catholics the obligation to respect the meaning of dogmas as determined once and for all by the Church.

The first to make use of such an approach and pay the price for it was Ignaz von Döllinger. Professor of Church History at the University of Munich (1826-1871) and president of the Bavarian Academy of Sciences (1873-1890), he was excommunicated in 1871 because he rejected the new dogmas on primacy and papal infallibility. He was a passionate reader, as well as a confidant, of his contemporary Möhler, and from that first generation of *Tübinger* he assimilated the essential characteristics of doing theology: an independent attitude with respect to the dominant curialism in Catholic seminaries ("We are university professors and not simple sacristans who carry out the orders", the founder of the Tübingen school Johann Sebastian Drey loved to repeat); the desire to deal with some profound issues of modernity, such as the need for critical knowledge of Christianity as history; and the belief that a rational demonstration of dogmatic faith was possible.[4]

The question of the reunification of the churches, all condensed into a kernel of unionist thought, which had already developed during the 1860s, became a priority issue for Döllinger after the First Vatican Council and his excommunication.[5] He had already spoken about it at length in an 1861 book, *Kirche und Kirchen. Papstthum und Kirchenstaat*, and then in his famous speech on the past and present of Catholic theology, given in 1863 in Munich to a meeting of Catholic scholars. Both aroused the interest leading Oxford Movement theologians, in particular Edward Bouverie Pusey and Henry Parry Liddon, with whom he had been in contact since 1845. Reduced to its bare bones, Döllinger's thought was that the churches should make an effort, in a frank dialogue purified from historical misunderstandings, to bring the specificities of each doctrinal tradition back to a common denominator of universal value in time and space. Döllinger clarified his meaning in a series of lectures from 1872, *On the reunion of the Christian churches* (*Über die Wiedervereinigung der christlichen Kirchen*). The only condition for the churches' mutual recognition was their continuity, in doctrine and structure, with the apostolic church of the origins, which requested as a guarantee fidelity to "Sacred Scripture with the three ecumenical symbols, interpreted according to the doctrine of the church undivided of the first three centuries".[6] The ecclesiological model of a future reunited church was therefore, to use today's terminology, that of a reconciled diversity that found its unifying centre in the *unam sanctam catholicam et apostolicam* of the creed.

The echo of his lessons throughout Europe, further amplified by the status of a martyr to which the Roman excommunication had inevitably elevated him, convinced Döllinger to undertake the project that would forever link his name to the ecumenical cause: the convocation in Bonn of two conferences on union. The first was held between 12 and 14 September 1874 and brought together theologians from East and West, with a majority component of *high church* Anglicans and a discreet, but at times reluctant, Old Catholic and Orthodox presence. Roman Catholics were obviously absent, giving the meeting an essentially intra-Protestant nature. The second, which took place in August 1875, left the denominational composition of the previous one almost unchanged. Dominated by Döllinger's strong personality, both conferences unexpectedly ended up getting stuck on an issue that overshadowed all others: the *filioque*. The proposal put forward by Döllinger in the first meeting, in fact, envisaged that all the parties would come together and declare "illegitimate" the introduction of the *filioque* in the profession of faith perfected at the Council of Constantinople in 381, and that, in the interests of peace and unity, the conference would establish the restoration of the original formula of the creed, as it had been defined by the councils of the undivided church. A crossfire fell relentlessly on Döllinger's idea. The Anglicans said they were willing to make amends for the ways in which the *filioque* was introduced definitively in 1014 by Pope Benedict VIII, but they refused to expunge from the creed a formula which had already been widespread in the West for centuries and fully conformed to the faith believed by the undivided church of the first centuries. The Orthodox, for their part, firmly rejected any downward compromise. This led to the drafting of a provisional declaration in which the introduction of the *filioque* into the creed was defined as "illegitimate" and in which the hope was expressed for a restoration of the original form of the text without sacrificing any doctrine expressed in the Western and Latin tradition of the church. The clarification of the passage relating to the procession of the Holy Spirit, however, was left to the following conference, where eight exhausting sessions and an additional day compared to the three initially planned were not enough to reconcile Orthodox and Protestants on a distinction that was very clear and eirenic only to the host: that between dogma and theological thinking.

It would not be wrong to say that part of the failure of Döllinger's initiative can be attributed precisely to the divisions that rose again around the question of the *filioque*, which continued to be discussed, not without polemical excess, even after the conclusion of the second and final conference in Bonn. On the one hand, Orthodoxy remained far from being conquered by that ecumenical vocation which would only redeem it from its long Ottoman captivity after the First World War, returning it to the world and to modernity. On the other, Anglo-Catholicism was becoming rigid in the face of the request to repeal an ancient formula of faith, knowing full well that, to gain the sympathy of the Orthodox, it would have to definitively renounce that of the Roman Catholics, which it persisted in cultivating with impatient anticipation, even after the trauma of Newman's defection in 1845 and despite the burdens imposed by the dogma of the Immaculate Conception (1854) and papal infallibility

(1871).[7]

What remains is the fact that, by returning the fact of faith to the horizon of human history rather than to the authoritative body of the ecclesial magisterium, Döllinger had reached the *filioque*, as well as the question of Anglican ordinations and the cult of the saints, just a step away from a truth which only Christians two generations later would be able to fully accept, when for the twentieth-century theology, the idea that the theological-doctrinal dimension of faith plays its destiny in close symbiosis with the actual configuration of faith, would no longer be taboo for churches in history.

3. Anglican theology and the Chicago-Lambeth Quadrilateral (1886-1888)

When at the end of the nineteenth century a rarefied desire for unity began to thicken in the institutional fabric of the churches, documents became the starting-point or the goal of any dialogue initiative. In the Lambeth Quadrilateral, the important declaration that the Anglican Communion adopted in 1888 to encourage ecumenical dialogues with other Christian traditions, the Nicene Creed, "as the sufficient statement of the Christian faith", appeared second in a list of four points, preceded by the Holy Scriptures, "as containing all things necessary to salvation", and accompanied by the apostolic creed "as the baptismal symbol". Third in the list came the two sacraments instituted by Christ, that is, baptism and the Lord's Supper, and finally the episcopate, "locally adapted in the methods of its administration to the varying needs of the nations and peoples called of God into the Unity of His Church".[8]

Envisaged as a condensation of traditional Anglican theology upon which to base, at a national level, forms of union with the Evangelical and Non-Conformist churches of the United Kingdom, the Quadrilateral was again proposed, in a reduced version, as a *companion* to the famous *Appeal to All Christian People*, a universal call to penance and contrition for the carnage of war that Christians had failed to stop at the 1920 Lambeth Conference. However, the roots of this first manifesto of Anglican ecumenical theology must be sought in the past and on the other side of the Atlantic.

The Lambeth Quadrilateral had in fact been born in Chicago two years earlier, in 1886, when the House of Bishops of the Protestant Episcopalian Church in the United States adopted a very similar declaration, mainly the result of the theological developments of William Reed Huntington. Thirty years earlier, this shy and influential Massachusetts theologian, tormented by the urge to heal the wounds left by the civil war that ended in 1865, had published his most important work, *The Church Idea. An Essay toward Unity*, which contained a perfect distillation of what would become the ecumenical flag of the Anglican Communion. According to Huntington, the perimeter of a united church, albeit still on a national basis, had to be delimited by four pillars: 1) Sacred Scripture; 2) the Nicene-Constantinopolitan symbol of faith; 3) the sacraments of baptism and the eucharist; 4) the episcopate as the cornerstone of ecclesial governance.

These were ideas that Huntington had assimilated directly from the Tractarian Movement, when as a young man, during a trip to England, he had the opportunity to meet John Keble, who with Newman and John Hurrell Froude, had been part of the first generation of Tractarians born and raised according to the clerical traditionalism that reigned at Oriel College in the University of Oxford.[9] Although by Huntington's maturity the Tractarian Movement had already lost the cohesion of its beginnings, and the historical reality of England was profoundly different from that which in the second and third decades of the century had triggered the public battles of these partisans of the Anglican establishment, the spirit and founding values of this tradition were still alive in its followers.[10] In the genetic makeup of the Tractarians there was first of all the idea of the church as a divinely constituted supernatural society and, in particular, of the Church of England as a national and reformed expression (in the sense of distinct from Rome) of the authentic universal Catholic church, an emanation of Christ and custodian of the apostolic faith. The theory of Anglican catholicity, so decisive for the development of what would be defined as branch theory, derived directly from the Caroline divines of the seventeenth century. Against any form of openness to the new political and religious scenarios produced by the revolutionary turbulence of that period, they had advocated a mystical-sacramental vision of the Anglican church as a branch of the universal church in which apostolicity was preserved intact in the uninterrupted succession of its bishops and in fidelity to the doctrine of the primitive church contained in the Nicene Creed and sanctioned by the first ecumenical councils.[11] This concept, albeit with significant distinctions, would remain lodged at the heart of an "orthodox" thought that reached from the golden age of the Stuarts to the Victorian age, where a generation of high churchmen judged the misfortune of a modern parliamentary culture based on values of pluralism and tolerance as the return effect of the great traumas of the seventeenth and eighteenth centuries, from Erastianism to Jacobinism across the Channel, passing through Puritanism, natural law and the Glorious Revolution.

Overseas, what was threatening the churches was certainly not a reformist political culture anxious to welcome the secularising pressures coming from below. The breakdown of the constitutional axis between church, monarchy, and Parliament was a concern unknown to the Episcopalians of America, but the demands of the Tractarian movement equally profoundly fertilised Anglicanism in the United States as the cause of Huntington well demonstrates.[12] The recovery of the foundations of the Christian faith and the vindication of the Catholic continuity of the Anglican tradition were in fact functional to redeeming the Episcopalian Church from its elitist condition and its colonial past, which made it a weak minority in the face of the blaze of the second great evangelical awakening, and gave it a chance to form the fragmented North American denominationalism into a national church with an inclusive character that would heal the country's political and religious fractures.

Taking for granted the pillar on Sacred Scripture as the sole and normative source of the Christian faith, especially given that at the start of ecumenism only Protestant churches spoke to each other, of the three remaining pillars that kept the Lambeth Quadrilateral standing, that of the Creed of Nicaea and Constantinople was certainly the least problematic and perhaps, in the eyes of a casual observer, the most obvious. Instead, its presence in that document-manifesto already indicated well in advance what would be the criterion that in the heart of the following century would guide the ecumenical movement through a season full of promises: that of bringing the churches back to converge on what remained shared of the apostolic faith in order to extinguish conflicts, especially those of an historical nature, removing the oxygen and fuel which allowed them to burn.

Translated by Patricia Kelly

Notes

1. Cfr. Johannes Oeldemann's contributon further in this issue.
2. Michel Fédou, "Scholarship and Unity in the 19th and 20th Century: Johann Adam Möhler and Adolf von Harnack Compared", in Luca Ferracci (ed.), *A History of the Desire for Christian Unity. Ecumenism in the Churches (19th–21st Century)*, Vol. I, Leiden: Brill, 2021, 300–319.
3. Johann Adam Möhler, *Symbolism. Or Exposition of the doctrinal differences between Catholics and Protestants as evidenced by their symbolical writings*, trans. J.B. Robertson. New York: Edward Dunnigan, 1844, p. 93.
4. Cf. Abraham Peter Kustermann, "La prima generazione della 'Katholische Tübinger Schule' tra rivoluzione e restaurazione", *Cristianesimo nella storia* 12/3 (1991), 489–526.
5. Franz Xaver Bischof, "Ignaz von Döllinger and the Bonn Reunion Conferences of 1874–1875", in Luca Ferracci (ed.), *A History of the Desire for Christian Unity*, Vol. I, 171–196.
6. Ignaz von Döllinger, *Über die Wiedervereinigung der christlichen Kirchen. Sieben Vorträge gehalten zu München im Jahr 1872*, Nördlingen: C.H. Beck, 1888, 139. The three symbols Döllinger referred to were the Nicene-Constantinopolitan Creed, the Apostles' Creed, and what has been handed down as the Athanasian Creed.
7. Mark Chapman, *The Fantasy of Reunion. Anglicans, Catholics and Ecumenism, 1833-1882*, Oxford: Oxford University Press, 2014.
8. R. Coleman (ed.), *Resolutions of the Twelve Lambeth Conferences (1867-1988)*, Anglican Book Centre, Toronto 1992, 13. Cf. Paul Avis, "The Origins of Anglican Ecumenical Theology, the Chicago-Lambeth Quadrilateral, and the Question of Anglican Orders, in Luca Ferracci (ed.), *A History of the Desire for Christian Unity*, Vol. I, 264–299.
9. Peter Nockles, "Newman and the Oxford Movement: A Prehistory of Ecumenism (1833–1870)", in Luca Ferracci (ed.), *A History of the Desire for Christian Unity*, Vol. I, 132–163.
10. Peter Nockles, *The Oxford Movement in Context. Anglican High Churchmanship 1760-1857*, Cambridge: Cambridge University Press, 1994.
11. Cf. Peter Nockles, "Anglicanism "Represented" or "Misrepresented", Evangelicalism, and History: The Controversial Use of the Caroline Divines in the Victorian Church of England", in Sheridan Gilley (ed.), *Victorian Churches and Churchmen*, Woodbridge/Rochester: Catholic Record Society publications, 2004, 308–369.
12. George E. DeMille, *The Catholic Movement in the American Episcopal Church*, Philadelphia: Church Historical Society, ²1950.

"Confessing the One Faith"
The contribution of a Faith and Order study to the anniversary of the Council of Nicaea

JOHANNES OELDEMANN

On the occasion of the anniversary of the Council of Nicaea, this article recalls a study document published in 1991 by the Faith and Order Commission, which offers an ecumenical explication of the Nicene-Constantinopolitan Creed. The context and progress of the study project as well as the methodology and content of the resulting study document are described, before the reception of this text is presented, its strengths and weaknesses analyzed and the challenges for the forthcoming anniversary of the Council identified.

The 6th World Conference on Faith and Order, which will take place in October 2025 under the motto 'Where Now for Visible Unity?', will focus on three main topics: faith, unity, and mission. Reflection on what unites us in faith and how we can overcome the differences in formulating our faith has shaped the history of Faith and Order since its inception in 1927. This article recalls a project of the Faith and Order Commission in the decade from 1982 to 1993. It was a study aimed at an ecumenical explication of the Apostolic faith as it is confessed in the Nicene-Constantinopolitan Creed (381). Looking back serves to take advantage of the results and findings of this project on the way to the 6th World Conference on Faith and Order.

1. Context and progress of the study project

Following *Baptism, Eucharist, and Ministry* (BEM), the Faith and Order Commission decided at its meeting in Lima in 1982 to address the significance of the Nicene Creed for ecumenism. The 1983 General Assembly of the World Council of Churches (WCC) in Vancouver mandated the newly formed commission to make this topic a priority of its upcoming working period. The project began with three ecumenical consultations, each on one article of the Creed, which were organized in Kottayam (India), Chantilly (France) and Kinshasa (Zaire) in 1984/85. Based on this preliminary work, the Steering Committee[1] of the study project drew up a first draft text, which was adopted and released for publication in August 1987. This first version of the study document was entitled "Confessing One Faith".[2]

In the following three years, the Secretariat of Faith and Order collected the reactions, comments, and proposed amendments to this first draft from ecumenical institutes, theological faculties, and study groups. At the same time, a second series of international consultations took place in which various aspects of the Creed were discussed: the doctrine of creation, Christology, ecclesiology, and pneumatology. At the 1989 plenary meeting of the Faith and Order Commission in Budapest (Hungary), the comments received were analyzed and a corresponding revision of the study was commissioned. At its meeting in Dunblane (Scotland) in August 1990, the Standing Commission of Faith and Order received the revised version and approved it for publication. This revised version was published under the title "Confessing the One Faith".[3] The 5th World Conference on Faith and Order in Santiago de Compostela in 1993 marked the conclusion of this study project.[4]

The study project on the apostolic faith did not receive the attention it deserved in the member churches and in the ecumenical audience at that time. There are two main reasons for this, which can be found in the historical context: Firstly, attention in the WCC at this time was focused primarily on the "Conciliar Process for Justice, Peace and Integrity of Creation", which found a broad resonance in the member churches and in numerous ecumenical assemblies. Secondly, the attention of the wider public focused on the social and political upheavals in Eastern Europe that led to the collapse of the communist regimes. As a result, questions of social ethics and the responsibility of the churches to society took center stage, while theological issues, such as those addressed in the study document "Confessing the One Faith", receded into the background of the ecumenical debate.

2. Methodology and content of the study document

The study project "Confessing the One faith" aimed at an ecumenical interpretation of the apostolic faith "to indicate the relevance of basic convictions of the Christian faith in the face of some particular challenges of our time and world".[5] The original wording of the Nicene-Constantinopolitan Creed (381) served as the reference text. The common explication was only one step in a threefold process, including mutual recognition and common witness as two supplementary steps.

The study document is divided into three parts, which are based on the three articles of the Creed. Each part comprises three or four sections in which the main themes of the respective article are addressed. Each section begins with introductory reflections in which fundamental challenges of the present are named. This is followed by the text of the Creed, quoting the relevant passages from the Nicene Creed and the Apostles' Creed, as well as explanations of the terminology and the foundations of the Creed in the biblical witness. This is followed by the 'Explication for today', in which the study document links the statements of the Creed with the challenges of the present and demonstrates their significance for today's understanding of faith. At various points, commentaries are inserted into the text in which controversial aspects are addressed. The document is quite comprehensive with 279 paragraphs (a good 100 pages in the printed version). A glossary in the appendix explains specialized theological terms such as 'apokatastasis', 'epiclesis', or 'filioque', which indicates that the commission intended the text to be received in wider circles. However, the language is so specific that prior theological knowledge is required in order to engage with the document.

2.1 The first article: We Believe in One God
The first main part of the study document deals with the belief in God as the one God, the Father Almighty and the Creator. The *Explication for today* combines basic convictions of Western theology (e.g., "Economic

and eternal Trinity is but one reality"[6]) with those of Eastern theology, like the monarchy of the Father as "eternal source of that living Trinitarian communion".[7] The text deals in detail with the challenges posed to the Christian belief in God by atheism and secularism and specifies the foundations for dialogue with other religions and beliefs. The second section deals with what it means when God is referred to as 'Father' and 'Almighty'. Remarkably, the text emphasizes "that this language neither attributes biological maleness to God nor implies that what we call 'masculine' qualities, assigned only to men, are the only characteristics belonging to God".[8] The Commission refers to female images to describe God in the biblical tradition (No. 43, 52) and mentions in a commentary that in some churches there is discussion about whether God can also be addressed as 'our mother', but ultimately makes a clear plea: "We may not surrender the names Father and Son."[9] In view of the characterization of God as 'Pantocrator' (Almighty), the question of theodicy is addressed as a critical question about God's omnipotence (No. 60), although the text only goes into this in more detail later in connection with the interpretation of Christ's suffering. The third section of the first article deals with the understanding of God as Creator. In the *Explication for today*, the text emphasizes the responsibility of human beings as "stewards of creation" (No. 85) and concludes by formulating an "ethics of creation". What is remarkable about the entire interpretation of the first article of faith is that the connection between the oneness of God and God's Trinitarian existence and work is repeatedly emphasized (Nos. 10, 49, 75, 89). The confession of the one God, who in Christ has reconciled the world to Godself and gives new life to it through the Holy Spirit, appears at the beginning and the end of the interpretation of the first article of the Creed (Nos. 6 and 89).

2.2 The second article: We Believe in One Lord Jesus Christ
The interpretation of the second article explicates fundamental aspects of Christology and soteriology in three sections: "Incarnate for Our Salvation", "Suffering and Crucified for Our Sake", and "Risen to Overcome all Evil Powers". The idea of pre-existence and the doctrine of incarnation of the Son of God are named as challenges for the belief in Christ in the present day. In explaining the text of the Creed, the study

document only briefly addresses the term '*homoousios*' and the debate with Arius, while the foundation in the biblical witness is broadly developed. Hermeneutical questions are also addressed: "The modern approach of historical exegesis need not exclude the patristic 'confessional' approach nor does the latter exclude the analysis of the growth of the Christological tradition. The two approaches are compatible and may even enrich each other".[10] In the *Explication for today*, the study document interprets in detail the understanding of sonship and the role of the Holy Spirit in the incarnation, but also addresses Mary's virginity and the confession of her as Mother of God (*Theotokos*).

In the second section, the document deals with the suffering and death of Jesus. In the introductory paragraphs, the 'for us' is particularly emphasized, thus taking up a classical topos of Protestant theology. In the *Explication for today*, two aspects are particularly noteworthy: firstly, the text critically examines the question of whether the Jewish people can be blamed for the suffering and death of Jesus, and states in this regard: "His death did not put an end to Israel's election, but in the hands of God became a means to expand it into the election of Jews *and* Gentiles, of all humanity".[11] The second fundamental question addressed in the *Explication for today* is the question of theodicy. In this regard, the text notes: "In the suffering and cross of Jesus, God has taken upon himself in the person of his Son the condition of human death that is provoked by our sin and demonstrated his solidarity with human beings and his compassion for their suffering."[12]

The third section deals with the understanding of the resurrection and ascension of Jesus Christ. Regarding the understanding of the resurrection, the text refers to "signs of the resurrection" in the lives of men and women who follow the crucified one, and "in the witness of the many confessors and martyrs of every age".[13] The concluding commentary points out that confessing the kingdom of Christ "implies criticism of systems and ideologies [...] with the unmasking of the false claims to permanence made in every kind of imperialism".[14] This statement proves to be almost prophetic in view of current neo-imperialist endeavors, such as those observed in the Russian war against Ukraine.

2.3 The third article: We Believe in the Holy Spirit

With regard to the third article of the Creed, the document specifies many challenges, e.g. "the conflict between East and West as to the *filioque*; [...] the relation of the Holy Spirit to the prophecy of the Old Covenant and the gift of prophecy in the Church; the criteria for the discernment of the activity of the Spirit within the Church".[15] After a brief presentation of the biblical witness, which interestingly omits the passage where the 'Spirit of his Son' is mentioned (Gal 4:6), a detailed *Explication for today* follows, in which there are many comments addressing controversial issues. They concern, among other things, the work of the Holy Spirit outside the church, the understanding of the Holy Spirit as a 'feminine principle' in God, the understanding of charisms, and the relationship between the Son and the Spirit. With regard to the *filioque* issue, the text attempts to build a bridge between the Eastern and Western concepts, referring to the Greek terminology that distinguishes between the 'procession' and the 'breathing forth' of the Spirit, and underlines: "both agree today that the intimate relationship between the Son and the Spirit is to be affirmed without giving the impression that the Spirit is subordinated to the Son".[16]

The second section concerns the confession to the one, holy, catholic and apostolic Church. In the interpretation of the biblical witness, it is emphasized that, according to Paul, "the election of the Church of God in Jesus Christ does not undo the election of Israel".[17] The *Explication for today* starts by linking the Church to the Trinitarian communion. This idea, only briefly touched on here, was developed more broadly twenty years later by the Faith and Order Commission in its convergence document 'The Church: Towards a Common Vision'.[18] In the study document of 1991 three biblical terms for the Church (body of Christ, communion of saints, people of God) are interpreted before the section looks at the four essential attributes of the Church.

The third section deals with the understanding of baptism. The relationship between baptism and church membership is addressed as a problem that requires further discussion, as well as the unity of the three sacraments of initiation and the differences between a sacramental and a symbolic understanding of baptism. With regard to the relationship between baptism and the forgiveness of sins, the doctrine of justification is addressed. Here the document adopts, on the one hand, the results of the

German study on the condemnations of the Reformation era[19], published a few years before, and, on the other hand, anticipates formulations that can be found a few years later in the "Joint Declaration on the Doctrine of Justification". The Orthodox doctrine of 'theosis' is also addressed in this context, but not further elaborated on.

The last thematic section of the third article of faith concerns the understanding of the resurrection of the dead and the life of the world to come. With regard to the understanding of resurrection, the immortality of the soul and universal salvation ('*apokatastasis panton*') are addressed as controversial issues. The text concludes with emphatic statements on "Living our hope" (No. 274 et seq.), with which the document comes to an almost sermon-like conclusion.

3. Reception of the study project and perspectives for the future

Although it was a large-scale study project by the Faith and Order Commission that has been running for almost ten years, the response it has received in the member churches of the WCC and in the academic world has been comparatively small. As mentioned, there are internal (WCC agenda) and external (political situation) reasons for this. The reception in the academic world is limited to a few articles and one more extensive study. In the latter, Eeva Martikainen emphasizes a shift in the methodology of the study project from recognition to explication of the Creed, probably because a text "full of theological nuances can only with difficulty serve as a convergence document".[20] Some articles praise the text as "a milestone in the church history of this century"[21], while in others it is critically noted that it was obviously difficult to create "a reasonably homogeneous text from the very different drafts".[22] It is recognised that the study document identifies the current challenges for confessing the faith in today's world, but criticised that these challenges are subsequently not sufficiently addressed.[23] A review from a Pentecostal author praises the explanations about the charisms, but criticises that "latent restorationism resonates with sensitivities to doxological and confessional orientations".[24] It is regrettable that there are still no dissertations or comparable studies on the academic reappraisal of the study project, especially because a comparison of the first version published in 1987 with the final version published in 1991 would be worthwhile in order to work out the emerging shifts in emphasis.

The Commission on Faith and Order itself tried to promote reception by publishing a handout for group discussions on the Creed.[25] A study by the German Ecumenical Study Committee (DÖSTA) aims in the same direction.[26] These materials can be used for the forthcoming anniversary of the Council to draw attention once again to the importance of the Nicene Creed. Ecumenical exchange about *experiences* of faith, as practised in the "Global Christian Forum", for example, seems more important today than the joint elaboration of additional texts on the Creed.

Looking back, what are the strengths and weaknesses of the study document published in 1991? The strengths certainly include the fact that it clearly identifies the challenges of that time, shows the foundation of the Creed in the biblical witness and offers a compendium of various interpretations of the creedal propositions in different Christian traditions. The strong passages include statements on the relationship between Jews and Christians and on theodicy. One weakness of the document is that it primarily focuses on "classical" topics in the history of theology, while perspectives from the global South or from non-creedal churches are hardly included. "Far too little justice has been done as yet to the challenge of the far-reaching inculturation of the Christian faith in Africa, Asia and Latin America."[27] The fact that the *Explication for today* immediately follows on the summary of the biblical witness has the consequence that certain historical developments in the interpretation of the Creed are not sufficiently taken into account.

The forthcoming anniversary of the First Ecumenical Council provides a welcome opportunity to take up again the question of how the apostolic faith is understood today. "Nicaea 2025 may prove to be the path of the study's renaissance."[28] It is not about bringing together the now even richer material[29] in a new study project. It is more about encouraging the churches to take the second step originally associated with the project: to promote the recognition, re-appropriation, and familiarization of the Creed in the different churches, especially in those who are not regularly using the Nicene Creed in their services.

The challenges of today are different from those of the 1980s: It is about post-colonial perspectives in a post-secular age, in which digitalization and social networks enable the spread of 'fake news' and lead us into a 'post-truth' era characterized by growing social polarization and increasing international conflicts. The Christian Creed therefore faces the challenge of being perceived as more than just a partial claim to truth. At a time when – especially in the charismatic and evangelical sphere – more and more trans-denominational groups are emerging, it would be an intriguing and challenging project to interpret the Creed in such a way that it can also be understood and accepted in a 'post-denominational' age. The anniversary of the Council of Nicaea offers the opportunity to respond to this challenge.

Notes

1 Chaired by the Catholic theologian Jean-Marie Tillard OP, its members included Ulrich Kühn, Wolfhart Pannenberg, Mary Tanner, and the later Ecumenical Patriarch Bartholomew.
2 Confessing One Faith: Towards an Ecumenical Explication of the Apostolic Faith as Expressed in the Nicene-Constantinopolitan Creed (381), Geneva: WCC, 1987 (FO Paper No. 140).
3 Confessing the One Faith: An Ecumenical Explication of the Apostolic Faith as it is Confessed in the Nicene-Constantinopolitan Creed (381), Geneva: WCC, 1991 (FO Paper No. 153).
4 Cf. On the Way to Fuller Koinonia. Official Report of the Fifth World Conference on Faith and Order, ed. by Th.F. Best and G. Gassmann, Geneva: WCC, 1994 (FO Paper No. 166), 237-244 (Report of Section II).
5 Confessing the One Faith, Introduction, No. 11.
6 Confessing the One Faith, No. 15.
7 Confessing the One Faith, No. 18.
8 Confessing the One Faith, No. 51.
9 Confessing the One Faith, No. 52.
10 Confessing the One Faith, No. 109.
11 Confessing the One Faith, No. 151.
12 Confessing the One Faith, No. 156.
13 Confessing the One Faith, No. 184.
14 Confessing the One Faith, Commentary to No. 191.
15 Confessing the One Faith, No. 195.
16 Confessing the One Faith, No. 210.
17 Confessing the One Faith, No. 223.
18 Cf. The Church: Towards a Common Vision, Geneva: WCC, 2013 (FO Paper No. 214), Chapter II: The Church of the Triune God (pp. 9-19).
19 Lehrverurteilungen – kirchentrennend? Vol. I: Rechtfertigung, Sakramente und Amt im Zeitalter der Reformation und heute, ed. by K. Lehmann und W. Pannenberg, Freiburg i.Br.: Herder / Göttingen: Vandenhoeck & Ruprecht, ³1988.
20 Eeva Martikainen, From Recognition to Reception: The Apostolic Faith and the Unity

of the Church in the World Council of Churches, Bern: Lang, 2002, 90.
21 E. Sturm, "Gemeinsam den einen Glauben bekennen: Zur ökumenischen Auslegung des Glaubensbekenntnisses von Nicäa-Konstantinopel", in: H. Horn (ed.), Didaskalos: Studien zum Lehramt in Universität, Schule und Religion. FS Gerhard J. Bellinger, Dortmund: Projekt, 1996, 73-93, here 74.
22 P.-W. Scheele, "Das ökumenische Zeugnis von der Gegenwart des Auferstandenen in der Kirche. Der Beitrag des ‚Faith and Order'-Projekts ‚Gemeinsam den einen Glauben bekennen'", in: J. Ernst / St. Leimengruber (eds.), Surrexit Dominus vere, Paderborn: Bonifatius, 1995, 317-328, here 319.
23 Cf. U. Link-Wieczorek, Gemeinsam denselben Christus entdecken? Überlegungen zum Studiendokument von Glauben und Kirchenverfassung „Gemeinsam den einen Glauben bekennen", in: Materialdienst des Konfessionskundlichen Instituts 49 (1998) 88-93.
24 H. D. Hunter, Confessing the One Faith (Review), in: Pneuma 14 (1992) 204-208, here 204.
25 Commission on Faith and Order, Towards Sharing the One Faith: A Study Guide for Discussion Groups, Geneva: WCC, 1996 (FO Paper No. 173).
26 Deutscher Ökumenischer Studienausschuss (DÖSTA), Wir glauben – wir bekennen – wir erwarten: Eine Einführung in das Gespräch über das Ökumenische Glaubensbekenntnis von 381, Eichstätt: Franz Sales, 1997.
27 M.E. Brinkman, The Will to Common Confession: The Contribution of Calvinist Protestantism to the WCC Study Project *Confessing the One Faith*, in: Louvain Studies 19 (1994) 118-137, here 132.
28 S. Beardsall, Living the Apostolic Faith Together Today, in: Ecumenical Review 75 (2023) 172-184, here 179.
29 Cf. for example the latest publication of the 'Altenberg Ecumenical Circle': H.-G. Link / J. Wohlmuth (eds.), Attraktive Fremdheit Gottes: Das ökumenische Bekenntnis von Nizäa-Konstantinopel (325-2025), Leipzig: EVA / Paderborn: Bonifatius, 2024.

Forum

Toward an understanding of Ratzinger's assertion of an "inalienable right of Greek thought to a place in Christianity"

FÁINCHE RYAN

This article examines core writings where Cardinal Ratzinger, later Pope Benedict XVI, explores the relationship between Greek thought and Christian faith. Particular consideration is given to his understanding of the significance of the Septuagint and of the formation of the classical symbols of faith, the Creeds. The argument is that, while Ratzinger undoubtedly argues for the authenticity and providential interaction of Christian tradition with Greek thought, his work can be read as nonetheless in principle open to an exploration of the pluralism of religions and the enrichment of interreligious dialogue.

What did the German theologian Cardinal Ratzinger, later Pope Benedict XVI, mean by his assertion that there was an "inalienable right of Greek thought to a place in Christianity"?[1] This article argues that Ratzinger's intention was not to assert that the Christian theological tradition, as formed in the context of Greek thought, is to be considered the unique and final expression of Christian faith. Rather, Ratzinger's concern was to defend the providential authenticity of Christian engagement with Greek thought. A further argument in this article is that the underlying theme of Ratzinger's work in this area is his concern for truth. For Ratzinger, the Christian tradition is to be understood as an exploration into truth. A lecture delivered in Hong Kong (1993) argues that it is from the perspective of the primacy of truth that issues of religious pluralism and interreligious dialogue are to be considered.² This article will examine core writings where Ratzinger explores the relationship between Greek thought and Christian faith, with special consideration given to his understanding of the significance of the Septuagint, and of the formation of the classical symbols of faith, the Creeds. The article concludes with a reference to the Anglican theologian, Rowan Williams, and his reflection on how the primacy of truth can be preserved in issues of religious pluralism and interreligious dialogue.

1. *Einführung in das Christentum*

Einführung in das Christentum, (*Introduction to Christianity*), Ratzinger's elucidation of the Apostles' Creed, first published in 1968 was republished with a new preface in 2000.³ In this work he seeks to articulate the foundations of Christian faith in the context of the contemporary world. The preface to the 1968 edition outlines Ratzinger's apprehension that the "real content and meaning of the Christian faith is enveloped today in a greater fog of uncertainty than at almost any earlier period in history." (31) In the background lies concern with what Ratzinger terms the dehellenisation of Christianity, which he interprets as implying a separation of faith and reason. It is in this context that Ratzinger writes of an "inalienable right of Greek thought to a place in Christianity." (78)⁴ This phrase occurs within a section of the book entitled *Belief in the World of Today:*

> This context is also the basis of an inalienable right of Greek thought to a place in Christianity. I am convinced that at bottom it was no mere accident that the Christian message, in the period when it was taking shape, first entered the Greek world and there merged with the inquiry into understanding, into truth. (78)

For the reprinted German edition of 2000 Ratzinger wrote a new preface. Thirty-two years after the initial publication Ratzinger reiterates his belief that the question about God, and about Christ as *logos*, should be the centerpiece of any introduction to Christian faith. (25) He notes that

"Ever since the Prologue to the Gospel of John, the concept of *logos* has been at the very center of our Christian faith in God. *Logos* signifies reason, meaning, or even 'word' – a meaning, therefore, that is Word, that is relationship, that is creative. The God who is *Logos* guarantees the intelligibility of the world [...] The world comes from reason and this reason is a Person, is Love – this is what our biblical faith tells us about God." (26)

His argument is clear. Since the 'beginning' of Christianity, as noted in John's Gospel, faith, love, and reason have been interwoven. This identification of Jesus as *logos* demonstrates, for Ratzinger, the interweaving of Christianity with its 'host' cultures, both the Hebrew Bible with its Wisdom tradition, and the Greek philosophical tradition. The argument of a Greek philosophical influence on John's gospel gives weight to the importance of deploying reason in the activity of Christian theology. Human reason leads us towards the mystery of God, and at once allows us to appreciate the mystery that God is. We are admonished to "trust the mystery of God in its incomprehensibility." (26) Ratzinger argues that Greek philosophy's search for truth has aided Christianity's journey into the mystery that is God, and that this has been providential. The argument of this article is that Ratzinger's overriding concern is not with proclaiming Greek philosophy as the only philosophy relevant for Christianity, but with a warning to keep truth at the centre.

2. The Harmony of Greek Thought and Biblical Faith
This belief in the inalienable right of Greek thought to a place in Christianity is evidenced in Ratzinger's reading of the Septuagint as the fruit of encounter between Hellenistic thought and Jewish faith. More than a word for word translation of the Hebrew text, the Septuagint provides independent textual witness, decisive for the birth and spread of Christianity. In continuity with this line of thought his Regensburg address (2006) notes "A profound encounter of faith and reason is taking place here, an encounter between genuine enlightenment and religion." [5]

Ratzinger contends that the imprint of the Greek spirit is particularly acute in the Septuagint translation of Exodus 3. This Hebrew text establishes the name Yahweh as the definitive name for the God of Israel. This mysterious name, Yahweh, is linked to the Hebrew root *hayah*, "to be". In this way Yahweh, the God of Abraham, Isaac and Jacob, is identified as "Being", as "I am". This way of thinking is used by the Fathers of the Church to develop a relationship between the God of biblical faith and the Greek idea of God as *esse subsistens*. Ratzinger is aware that scholars dispute this. This leads Ratzinger to ask if the God that names Godself Yahweh, the God that helps and is present, is "radically different from the *esse subsistens*, the absolute Being, that is discovered in the lonely silence of philosophical speculation." (130) Ratzinger suggests that it was likely that the scholars who translated "the Hebrew Bible into Greek were influenced by Greek philosophical thinking and interpreted the text from this angle." (118, 119) Influenced by the idea that the Hellenistic spirit and the faith of the Bible overlapped, these scholars, Ratzinger argues, built a bridge from the biblical concept of God over to the Greek thought, translating the 'I AM WHO I AM' of Exodus 3: 14 to 'I am he that is.' "The biblical name for God is here identified with the philosophical concept of God." (119) Here Ratzinger sees a deliberate connection being made by Christian faith with the God of the philosophers. Importantly he then proceeds to argue that purely philosophical thinking is transcended in Christian faith on two fundamental points: firstly, the philosophical God is essentially self-centered, thought contemplating itself, while the God of faith is basically relational, "the highest mode of Being includes the element of relationship" (148); secondly the philosophical God is pure thought, and so pure thought is deemed divine. In contrast the God of faith, "as thought, is also love ... to love is divine." (148)

Ratzinger's argument is that in the encounter of Greek thought with biblical faith, there was both a transformation of Greek thought and an exploration into the truth of biblical faith. For Ratzinger, John's gospel, influenced by the Wisdom literature and Deutero-Isaiah writings, makes the powerful 'I am' of Isaiah 43 the central formula of his Christology. The 'I am' of Exodus 3 and of Isaiah 43 is Jesus Christ. In John 17 Jesus is the revealer of the name of God, the one in whom the story of the burning bush (Exodus 3) attains its true meaning. Jesus Christ is 'I am' and Jesus Christ is the *logos* of God (John 1). (132) This term, *logos,* was current in both Greek and Hebrew thought. By its application to Jesus the concept *logos* no longer simply denotes that all being is permeated by meaning, it now signifies that all that is meant by *logos* is now present in this person Jesus. In this way Ratzinger argues for the authenticity of the contribution of the Hellenistic heritage to the articulation of the Gospel in the age of the Fathers of the Church. It is important to note that he views this enrichment as providential. It is in this context he speaks of an 'inalienable right' of Greek thought to Christianity.

3. The Creed

In a further development the conciliar *symbola* composed at the councils of Nicaea and Constantinople applied language and understanding to the baptismal confession of faith. Ratzinger argues that Greek philosophy provided a language capable of expressing the central truth of the faith, namely that 'I am' (Ex 3:14) is a name of Jesus, Son of God. The fruitfulness of Greek thought when combined with biblical faith is evidenced for example in the process of asserting the non-scriptural term, *homoousios*. Ratzinger suggests that here we again see the hand of providence. The encounter between the faith of the Bible and Greek philosophy, for Ratzinger, was truly providential.[6]

Ratzinger's concern is that truth must be the concern of Christianity. The binding force of the Creeds is in their truth, not because of the language developed and adapted to express this truth. The faith of the Church and of its members existed before theologies, before Creeds. The faith of the Church is a commitment to a truth received and lived in its sacraments and prayer. That it found expression in words is key to its survival. It is because of the truth that the Creeds seek to express that they are binding. This is what Ratzinger intends to mean when he states "[w]ith that, the wording of the dogma was to all intents and purposes settled." (183) Ratzinger is aware that while faith has definitive statements, termed dogma and Creed

> this does not mean that these formulas cannot open further in the course of history and thus be understood in fresh ways. ... it does mean that in the course of this understanding and maturing the unity of what is understood neither can be nor may be destroyed. (265)[7]

This demonstrates that while Ratzinger strenuously and articulately defends the "inalienable right of Greek thought to a place in Christianity," the door is never firmly shut to fresh ways of understanding the Creeds. The providential articulation of the faith in the age of the Fathers and in the formation of the Creeds, while having real authority, comparable to that of the Septuagint, does not close off but rather can be a resource for further developments from different cultural contexts.

4. The Truth of Christian Tradition and the Challenge of Cultures

The 1993 Hong Kong paper, mentioned earlier, was delivered by Ratzinger at a meeting with Presidents of the Doctrinal Commissions of the Asian Episcopal Conferences. The paper was entitled *Christ, Faith and the Challenge of Cultures*.[8] In this paper Ratzinger argued that the concept of inculturation was a cul-de-sac. Inculturation, he said, presupposes a faith stripped of culture being transplanted into another different culture, and there is no such thing as a faith stripped of culture. In response he coined a new phrase: 'interculturation'. Ratzinger's point is that the Gospel is not an abstract essence to be clothed, as it were, with the "foreign" culture into which it was being proclaimed. The Gospel always presents itself as shaped by a particular historical culture, so that evangelization always involves an encounter with other cultures that are more or less open to receive God's self-revelation, Jesus Christ.

When Ratzinger considers the meaning of cultures in a way that is mutually enriching and not just superficially linked one to another, he says:

> The medium that brings them together can only be the shared truth about the human, which necessarily brings into play the truth about God and reality as a whole. The more human a culture is, the greater it is, the more it will speak to truth which was formerly closed to it and the more it will be able to assimilate truth and itself be assimilated by truth. [9]

In this encounter, metaphysics cannot be avoided. Cultures can meet and enrich one another because within each culture humankind is concerned with truth, the truth of human existence. The core preoccupation of Ratzinger is truth and the indefeasibility of the Christian exploration into truth. He sees Christian faith's self-understanding as an interlocutor in the search for truth between and within cultures. As with his consideration of Greek thought and Christianity it is once again the openness to the search for truth that is understood as the medium within which intercultural interaction can take place. The other culture's philosophical assumptions will inevitably be purified and transformed to express the perennial truth of revealed faith. In the end, new expressions should transcend any particular culture. To the extent that it articulates the truth, the new expression can speak to people of all cultures since it, though richer, will be in profound harmony with what was previously defined as dogma. It is in this above sense that the Creed can be said to be 'binding' on other cultures – i.e., in so far as the truth is binding on all. At the center of Ratzinger's thought stands the foundational understanding that Jesus is the Word, the *logos* and the truth of God.

There is clear tension here. Ratzinger, in his work, is open to interculturality, to new expressions of the truth of faith. At the same time he remains faithfully adamant that if Jesus of Nazareth really is the incarnate meaning of history, the *Logos*, the self-manifestation of truth itself, it "is then clear that this truth is the place where everyone can be reconciled and nothing loses its own worth and dignity."[10]

5. Conclusion

Ratzinger's work in this area is best considered as a creative tension that can be the stimulus for further theological exploration. One such line of exploration is found in the work of Rowan Williams. In an essay entitled *Trinity and Pluralism*, discussing the work of Raimundo Panikkar, Williams notes "that to the extent that the relationship of Spirit to Logos is still being realised in our history, we cannot ever, while history lasts, say precisely all that is to be said about Logos."[11] Ratzinger would not disagree. Ratzinger's thought, while undoubtedly being in defence of the authenticity and providentiality of the interaction of Christian tradition with Greek thought - "I am convinced that at bottom it was no mere accident that the Christian message, in the period when it was taking shape, first entered the Greek world and there merged with the inquiry into understanding, into truth" - can nonetheless be read as in principle open to an exploration of the pluralism of religions and the enrichment of interreligious dialogue.

Notes

1. 'das durch nichts aufzuhebende Recht des Griechischen im Christlichen.' Joseph Cardinal Ratzinger, *Einführung in das Chrisentum*, Munich: Kösel-Verlag, 1968, 51.
2. Joseph Card. Ratzinger, *Christ, Faith and the Challenge of Cultures* (1993) https://www.vatican.va/roman_curia/congregations/cfaith/incontri/rc_con_cfaith_19930303_hong-kong-ratzinger_en.html [16 June 2024].
3. References in this article are from the English translation, *Introduction to Christianity*. Translated by J.R. Foster and Michael J. Miller, San Francisco: Ignatius Press, Communio Books, 2004. Henceforth reference to page numbers in this book are made in the body of the text.
4. The term 'inalienable right' is the translation given of *aufzuhebende Recht*.
5. Pope Benedict XVI, *Faith, Reason and the University. Memories and Reflections* (Regensburg lecture) https://www.vatican.va/content/benedict-xvi/en/speeches/2006/september/documents/hf_ben-xvi_spe_20060912_university-regensburg.html [7 March 2024]
6. See also Joseph Ratzinger, *Truth and Tolerance: Christian Belief and World Religions*, San Francisco: Ignatius Press, 2004, 95.
7. In a paper delivered in 1965 to a state academy in Nordrhein-Westfallen he noted that "In every dogma there is necessarily an incongruence between the word, the language, in which it is said, and the reality, which it tries to express and which it can never fully capture" *Das Problem der Dogmengeschichte in der Sicht der katholischen Theologie*, Cologne and Opladen: Westdeutscher Verlag, 1966, 25.
8. Joseph Card. Ratzinger, *Christ, Faith and the Challenge of Cultures* http://www.vatican.va/roman_curia/congregations/cfaith/incontri/rc_con_cfaith_19930303_hong-kong-ratzinger_en.html [16 June 2024].
9. http://www.vatican.va/roman_curia/congregations/cfaith/incontri/rc_con_cfaith_19930303_hong-kong-ratzinger_en.html Section 2. [16 June 2024].
10. http://www.vatican.va/roman_curia/congregations/cfaith/incontri/rc_con_cfaith_19930303_hong-kong-ratzinger_en.html Section 3. [16 June 2024.
11. Rowan Williams, 'Trinity and Pluralism' in *On Christian Theology*, Oxford: Blackwell, 2000, 167–180, here 178.

Nicaea as Symbol of Faith and Symbol of Tragedy?

STEVEN BATTIN

This article draws a connection between the victory of Nicaea in 325 and the ongoing tragedy of coloniality for indigenous peoples and their cultures beginning in 1492. It argues that Nicaea has a "tragedy side" that reverberates through Christian history, contributing in its own way to colonial modernity's penchant for refusing dialogue with the indigenous Other and denying to the indigenous Other epistemic and spatial autonomy.

1. Introduction

At the dawning of modernity, two months after Columbus' return from his first voyage to the lands that would come to be called the Americas, Pope Alexander VI issued the papal bull *Inter Cetaera Divinae*. In it, he writes to the soon-to-be Spanish colonizers: "by the bowels of mercy of our Lord Jesus Christ we especially enjoin that, as you intend to carry out such an expedition with a willing mind and zeal for orthodox faith, you should and must cause peoples dwelling in those islands and continents to accept the Christian religion."[1] Alexander's statement seamlessly weaves together not simply Christian faith, but "orthodox" Christian faith, with the injunction to compel the Americas' indigenous peoples into the "orthodox" version of Christian religion. Admittedly, many elements go into the common orthodoxy of Western Christian churches (e.g., salvation through Christ and from sin), but some would say *primus inter pares* is God as Trinity. Thus, it is Nicene-Constantinopolitan-Chalcedonian Christians who embark on voyages across the Atlantic not so that Christ's name might be invoked in the "New World" independently of the evangelizer's ecclesial affiliation, but so that the evangelized will be forced to submit to an invading people's "orthodox faith."

In this article, therefore, I want to reflect on the 1700th anniversary of Nicaea in light of the not-so-long ago 500th anniversary of the European Christian invasion of the Americas. To do so, I contend, requires retelling Nicaea's story not only as triumph, but also tragedy. Furthermore, I suggest that tragedy as a mode of narrative recollection of historical events is integral to decolonial projects in general and is, therefore, particularly salient for the Church's participation in what Enrique Dussel has called the "unfinished project of decolonization." Tragedy, in this sense, is a counteractive force to romantic narratives of "victory" that occlude perception of the great harm done in achieving such victories.

In the first two sections I turn to two indigenous thinkers to briefly explicate the concepts of coloniality and tragedy, the two poles of theoretical framework for reflecting on Nicaea's past victory in relation to colonization and coloniality. In the following two sections I trace out the "tragedy side" of Nicaea as a way of identifying the resonances of that tragedy within the modern/colonial world for reflection in decolonization struggles today.

2. The Relationship between Christianity and Modernity/ Coloniality

Aiban Wagua, an indigenous Kuna theologian and poet from Panama, and a leading proponent for intercultural bilingual education among indigenous peoples of Abya Yala, contributed to the 1990 issue of *Concilium* dedicated to victims of the colonization of Latin America, from 1492-1992. A main point of his article is that the atrocities of settler-colonialism are not in the past; they are ongoing: "Our grandparents know many stories of the European invasion, but it means much more to them when these stories are put in the present bloody context of our communities; they set fire to the trunk, and the tree is still painfully burning."[2] Thinking from modernity's underside, Wagua gave voice to a key insight later taken up by Latin American and Latinae decolonial scholars: Colonialism is not an event by which modernity was inaugurated; rather, it is the structure of modernity. Therefore, we may say, in congruence with decolonial theorists, that a better way of naming modernity, from the perspective and experience of its underside, is coloniality.

What, then, of the relationship between Christianity and coloniality? First to be noted is that Christianity predates modernity/coloniality. Christian theology and worldview, particularly the worldview of Christendom, contributed to modernity/coloniality. Christendom and the segments of Christianity that bear its spirit are at odds with modernity but in perfect alignment with coloniality. In its traversal across the Atlantic, the Carolingian imperialism constitutive of western European Christendom was transformed into the colonialism of settler Christianity in the "New World." Christendom's transatlantic reconfigurations were momentous; for as Anibal Quijano notes, "as the centuries went by, the New World became the pattern, the model of the entire world-system."[3] A second point is that if there is a Christian modernity, there is also a Christian coloniality. The first entails Christianity's experience of and adjustment to modernity; the second indicates Christianity's complicity in the political and epistemic domination of non-Western indigenous Others[4] and their forced readjustment to the "logics" and "norms" of orthodox Christianity. It is, then, no surprise that as Christian modernity in the West often defines itself in either hostile or conciliatory relation to secular modernity, from modernity's underside, coloniality can appear under the aegis of either the secular or the Christian, or both at the same time.

3. Narrating Modernity/Coloniality and Christian Coloniality as Tragedy

Having posited a distinction between modernity/coloniality and Christian coloniality as well as their inseparability, we now turn to an important insight from Native American theologian George "Tink" Tinker, a member of the Osage Nation (a Midwestern American tribe of the Great Plains) and an ordained Lutheran minister. In an interview with the Iliff School of Theology, where he taught for 32 years, Tinker shared his approach to teaching students preparing for ministry. He contends that they should "understand there is a recipe there [in Christian ministry] for doing great harm in the world, even as they "think" only about accomplishing good and great things."[5] Crucial to this apperception of harm, even as an unintended consequence of a perceived good, is an awareness of romance and tragedy as operative modes of narrating past, present, and future. For Tinker, narratives of victory and overcoming function as "romantic façades" that cover over the evitable and "reversible" circumstances of history, whereas tragedy promotes a vigilant perception of harm in the past and present and cultivates an aspiration to prevent it in the future. Tinker maintains that it is imperative to "get at the underside of the history of Christianity to demonstrate how Christianity in the modern world has marched hand in hand with European Christian colonialism."[6] As Tinker reminds us,

> the spread of Christianity follows the spread of Christian conquest from the fifteenth century until now… [the spread of Christianity] is not just a wonderful thing…in fact, it has its underside, its tragedy side. . .Indian communities have been decimated by…churches, whose first and foremost aim was to destroy Indian cultures and replace it with a Christian culture. That's not an unmitigated good. In fact, it makes life very difficult for young men (like I was) and women trying to reclaim the American Indian self.[7]

For Tinker, there is a danger in Christian modernity narrating its missionary triumph romantically, and thus recapitulating the harms of Christian coloniality. To break from continuously repeating Christianity's colonial past in the ever-present moment of coloniality—that is, to participate in the project of decolonization—requires narrating the "tragedy side" of Christian modernity.

If, as Pope Francis has said, reality is best seen and understood from the periphery rather than from the center,[8] then, following Tinker's lead, modernity/coloniality and Christian coloniality is best viewed through the lens of tragedy rather than romance. So important is this lens of tragedy for Tinker that he stresses the point, saying, "theology is tragedy, history is tragedy, American history is tragedy, Christian history is tragedy. It's not just 'things keep getting better and better.'"

With this last point, Tinker invites us to go further, to think not only of coloniality as tragedy and the tragedy side of "successful" evangelization in the Americas but the tragedy side of Christian history and ecclesial identity formation prior to its crossing the Atlantic. We must, therefore, ask: Is there a tragic side to the premodern "orthodox faith" Pope Alexander VI enjoined conquistador's and their accompanying missionaries to impose—by violence, if necessary—on the indigenous peoples of the Americas?

What, if any, is Nicaea's role in this tragedy of orthodox Christianity? And how does this intra-Christian tragedy reverberate to 1492 and into the present?

4. Toward Narrating the "Tragedy Side" of Nicaea

The road to Nicaea as tragedy is circuitous, but thinking about the Symbol of Nicaea in relation to violent evangelization and ongoing coloniality enables us to ask a pointed question: Why, if Nicaea is so central to faith identity, does it seem to carry no potential for motivating interventions against atrocities throughout Christian history, and particularly the atrocities of coloniality in either its originary moment or today? The conquistadors, colonizers, and violent missionizing priests who Pope Alexander VI commissioned to conquer in the name of orthodox Christianity had no compunction about participating in exploitation, enslavement, and physical and cultural genocide of other human beings. The colonizer Christians doing this violence were going to Mass every Sunday and reciting the Nicene-Constantinopolitan Creed, yet nothing in the Creed gave them pause, at all. In fact, Las Casas recounts that when Fray Antonio de Montesinos preached against the colonizer's abuses of the Taíno peoples in light of the gospel, the colonizers accused the Dominicans of inventing a new, bizarre doctrine! Why, within the history of (compassionate) Christianity, does reflection on scripture or experience seem to ignite a desire for justice, whereas dogmas of tradition, such as the Nicene Symbol, do not appear as a source for forming a Christian conscience sensitive to the scandal of collective Christian participation in episodic or systemic harm against the Other?

Perhaps an insight from preeminent History of Christianity scholar Brian Daley SJ provides a clue. Commenting on why theoretical models of the trinity fail, he writes "our thought and speech about God as Trinity is not, in any sense, a theory or hypothesis intended to explain how God has touched us in history." Trinitarian speech "simply confesses, proclaims."[9] But I suspect he comes closer to the issue when he says orthodox trinitarian speech reveals "that statements about God as one substance and three *hypostases* are, first of all, boundary statements: statements that mark out, in the name of the community of Christian faith and worship, the limits of what represents biblical and ecclesial faith from what lies outside it."[10] The wording of Daley's comment both reveals and obscures. It reveals that the function of Nicaean trinitarian orthodoxy is demarcation. It obscures that the object of demarcation is not only a "what" but also a "who." In other words, Nicaean orthodoxy's function, within the life of the community, is to delimit who is "in" and who is "out."

I want to suggest that it is precisely around this issue of border construction and identity policing that the story of Nicaea's origin and triumph invite a narrative of tragedy. At first, an intra-Christian tragedy, but through the twists and turn of history, one indelibly connected to cataclysmic tragedy for millions of non-European, non-Abrahamic, non-state peoples throughout the world.

5. The Road to Nicaea: A Tragic Trajectory

The Council of Nicaea is commonly narrated as the victory of truth over error. In this vein, Athanasius calls the Symbol of Nicaea, "a true monument and token of victory against every heresy."[11] But was "heresy" the only thing defeated? Was something else lost in a controversy that, according to Eusebius, Constantine initially described as "intrinsically trifling and of little moment"?[12] I propose here that what was lost was the opportunity for Christianity to define itself as "pluriversal," to use a term from decolonial theory.

On the one hand, the ability of early Christianity to travel and adapt resulted in a sea of intra-Christian difference that carried the possibility of *"un mundo donde quepan otros mundos"* (a world where all worlds are included). A glimpse of this possibility appears in Justin Martyr's *Dialogue with Trypho*, when Justin mentions the existence of Christians outside his Logos-school—but perhaps in his own church! —who hold that Jesus "has a merely human origin."[13] Acknowledging this significant difference, he nevertheless includes them within the fold of those legitimately called Christian. Though they have a different "opinion" they coexist peacefully within the same ecclesial space as those whose "opinions" will later be called "orthodox."

On the other hand, it is clear from our earliest written testimonies that Christian communities had a sectarian inclination, and therefore an impulse to confrontation and exclusion. The sectarian inclination divides the world neatly into "us" and "them." It compels the drawing and maintaining of boundaries. It hyper-fixates on differences, great and small, essential and arbitrary. In terms of social psychology, this sectarian inclination correlates with processes of "moral exclusion." As described by social psychologist Susan Opotow, "Moral exclusion occurs when individuals or groups are perceived as outside the boundary in which moral values, rules and considerations of fairness apply."[14] I have talked about this phenomenon in more depth elsewhere,[15] but here I must mention one important sub-process of moral exclusion: Ingroup/outgroup categorization. This cognitive process is associated with ingroup bias; and studies have demonstrated that "even an arbitrary criterion for group formation, such as a person's preference for circles versus triangles, can trigger in-group biases in both groups."[16] Any difference, then, if associated with communal self-identity in a sectarian register, could trigger a cascade effect of boundary lines.

From the second half of the second century to Nicaea, the redlining impulse of sectarianism intensifies, narrowing the scope of intra-Christian fellowship. Thus, for example, by the second quarter of the third century, as attested in Novation's *On the Trinity* (30), Justin's fellow Christians-in-difference are labeled as "heretics," with whom there can be no communion. Dialogue and the possibility of fellowship with those who have an understanding of Christ based on more of a Judean-cultural synthesis have been foreclosed. The fertile possibilities of mutually coexisting and dialogical intra-Christian Otherness give way to the desire for dogmatic sameness. Moving along our timeline toward Nicaea, we see the cumulative effects of ingroup/outgroup categorization: the more sectarianized Christians tied philosophical speculation to Christian self-identity as such, the more fractious and bellicose the network of Christians and the emerging trinitarian orthodoxy would become—whether that trinitarian orthodoxy was "Arian" or "Athanasian."

A result of this trend, of which Nicaea may be seen as its symbolic highpoint, the post-Nicene Church was no longer capable of imagining communion inclusive of significant difference. Nicaea, then, is the victory of orthodoxy; but correlatedly, it is also, in a sense, the victory of the sectarian tendency for sameness and bellicosity over the cosmopolitan tendency for conviviality and communion. Which takes us to the main point: Nicaea, in light of this development, is a culmination in a regretful development of the exclusionary inclination that preceded it and accelerated after it. From this perspective, the Nicene Symbol represents not so much a turning point as a point of no return. The victory of Nicaea also has a "tragedy side."

Importantly for our consideration, the victory of Nicaean orthodoxy (even if the win had gone to Arius) was a tragedy for Christian intercommunal relations with the radically Other. As a marker of inclusion/exclusion, in the context of modernity/coloniality, the Symbol of Nicaea either directly or indirectly contributes to—or lacks theological capacity to engender mobilization against—coloniality.

6. Conclusion

There is a correlation between the tragedy of coloniality and the tragic side of Nicaea. But Nicaea is not the cause of coloniality; rather, it is, historically, a conditioning factor in the development of the attitude and epistemology that is constitutive of coloniality, in both its secular *and* Christian articulations. It is, as must be affirmed, an integral part of Pope Alexander's "orthodox" and violently evangelizing faith. What came to the Americas as part of orthodox faith, in its capacity as a carrier of a now militarized sectarian impulse, was a refusal to engage in dialogue. After all, what is there to learn from the Other outside the fold? Orthodox faith also brought across the Atlantic a particular theo-cultural synthesis that functions as the grammar of a universal Christianity, disallowing, as best it can, the inevitable difference and possible pluriversality that would emerge from the gospel's synthesis with the cultures of the radically Other. For those on modernity's underside, the abrogation of dialogue and denial of epistemic and spatial autonomy are constitutive features of modernity/coloniality; features that, sadly, trace their roots to Alexander's "orthodox faith." Moreover, the creed of Nicaea, in its original context, was understood as symbol, in the sense of a "token serving as proof of identity."[17] Nicaea is not only a symbol in the original sense, but also in the contemporary sense of a figure representing something other than or beyond itself. Nicaea in this sense can be seen as a signifier or synecdoche for characteristics of a colonizing orthodox Christian community of which Nicaea is a part but which could be analyzed apart from Nicaea. So, in the first sense, Nicaea is a symbol of the faith; in the second sense, Nicaea is a symbol of tragedy. I have presented here a necessarily periphrastic approach by which to problematize Nicaea in relation to Christian coloniality.

In commemorating the momentous Council that convened for three months in Nicaea in 325, perhaps we can be both celebratory and somber. As Paul enjoins us to "rejoice with those who rejoice and weep with those who weep" (Rom 12:15), it may be helpful, on such a jubilant occasion as Nicaea's 1700th anniversary, to remember those who, for 500 years, have wept and are still weeping. But they have also resisted and are still resisting the coloniality Western Christianity created, in part because of its own internal unresolved traumas. This resistance does not constitute a threat to "unity" or the "core" of Christian identity. Rather, it is an invitation to eschew the temptations to construct romantic façades that unhealthily protect orthodoxy from the darker, tragic side of its own history. Such a reckoning and repentance may be a necessary step for any orthodox Christian church to fully participate in the unfinished project of decolonization.

Notes

1 Pope Alexander VI, Papal Bull Inter Cetaera Divinae, par. 5.
2 Aiban Wagua, "Present Consequences of the European Invasion of America," 1492–1992: The Voice of the Victims, edited by Leonardo Boff and Virgil Elizondo, Concilium, no. 4 (1990), 47–56, here 48.
3 Anibal Quijano and Immanuel Wallerstein, "Americanicity as a Concept, or the Americas in the Modern World-System," International Social Science Journal 44.4 (1992), 459–557, here 549–550.
4 I am following Enrique Dussel's convention of capitalizing "Other" to signify the collective subjectivities whose radical difference from the European/Christian is covered over. Enrique Dussel, Invention of the Americas: Eclipse of the Other and the Myth of Modernity, translated by Michael D. Barber, New York: Continuum, 1995.
5 George Tinker, "Interview of Tink Tinker: Stir the Mud Up from the Bottom of the Pot. Illif School of Theology," at https://www.youtube.com/watch?v=ri2DJ_bI-p0A&t=354s&pp=ygUUZ2VvcmdlIHRpbmtlciwgaWxsaWY%3D.
6 Tinker, "Interview."
7 Tinker, "Interview."
8 Pope Francis in Antonio Spadaro, S.J., Wake Up the World! Conversations with Pope Francis about the Religious Life, translated from Italian by Fr. Donald Maldari S.J., La Civilta Cattolica, 2014.
9 Brian Daley, S.J., "Foreword" in Khaled Anatolios, Retrieving Nicaea: The Development and Meaning of Trinitarian Doctrine, Grand Rapids: Baker Academic, 2011, x.

10 Daley, "Forward," xiii.
11 Philip Schaff, History of the Christian Church, Volume 3: Nicene and Post-Nicene Christianity, A.D. 311-600, Grand Rapids: Christian Classics Ethereal Library, 542, at http://www.ccel.org/ccel/schaff/hcc3.html.
12 Eusebius, The Life of Constantine (Book 2), in Philip Schaff, Nicene and Post-Nicene Fathers Series 2, Vol 1, Grand Rapids: Christian Classics Ethereal Library, 1277, at http://www.ccel.org/ccel/schaff/npnf201.html.
13 Justin Martyr, Dialogue with Trypho, edited by Michael Slusser, translated by Thomas B. Falls, revised by Thomas P. Halton, Washington: Catholic University of America, 2003, 74
14 Susan Opotow, "Moral Exclusion and Injustice: An Introduction," Journal of Social Issues 46.1 (1990), 1–20, here 1.
15 Steven Battin, Intercommunal Ecclesiology: The Church, Salvation, and Intergroup Conflict, Eugene: Cascade, 2022, 56–80.
16 Joshua Goldstein, War and Gender: How Gender Shapes the War System and Vice Versa, Cambridge: Cambridge University Press, 2001, 225.
17 Henry Liddell and Robert Scott, A Greek-English Lexicon (English and Greek Edition), editors Robert McKenzie and Henry Jones, Oxford: Oxford University Press, 1990.

Contributors

GIACOMO FREDA CIVICO graduated in Archaeological Sciences from La Sapienza University, from where he also obtained a Master's Degree in Historical Sciences; he has been a doctoral student at the same university since November 2023, continuing his research on early Christianity among the Goths, the focus of his studies since his Master's thesis.
   Address: Viale Vaticano 67 00165, Rome, Italy
   Email: giacomo.fredacivico@uniroma1.it

BISHARA EBEID is Assistant Professor of Arabic Language and Literature at Ca' Foscari University of Venice. Specialized in Christian Arabic theology and literature he has published various contributions in this field like the monographs La tunica di Al-Masīḥ. La Cristologia delle grandi confessioni cristiane dell'Oriente nel X e XI secolo, Roma: Edizioni Christiana Orientalia, 2018; 2019; the critical edition of Elias of Nisibis. Commentary on the Creed (Tafsīr al-amānah al-kabīrah), with English translation and comments, CNERU-CEDRAC, Beyrouth, 2018.
   Address: Department of Asian and North African Studies Ca' Foscari University of Venice San Polo 2035, 30125 Venice, Italy
   Email: bishara.ebeid@unive.it

PAOLO ARANHA is a Church historian specialised in the early modern Catholic missions to India. He has published an Italian monograph on Latin Christianity in India during the sixteenth century and is preparing a comprehensive history of the Malabar Rites controversy. He studied in "La Sapienza" University (Rome) and the European University Institute (Florence). He worked at the Warburg Institute and the LMU (Munich). He is currently a fellow of the Istituto Italiano di Studi Germanici (Rome).
   Address: Via Leone IX, 3 00165 – Roma, Italia
   Email: paolo.aranha@gmail.com

AUSTIN JOHN MILLARES ORTINERO is a PhD researcher in

systematic theology at KU Leuven Belgium. He earned his Master's and Ecclesiastical Licentiate Degrees in Philosophy from the University of Santo Tomas, Manila, Philippines and his Advanced Research Master's and Ecclesiastical Licentiate Degrees in Theology from KU Leuven, Belgium. His incardination is the Archdiocese of Caceres.
   Address: KU Leuven, Faculty of Theology and Religious Studies, Sint-Michielsstraat 4 - box 3101, 3000 Leuven, Belgium
   Email: austinjohnmillares.ortinero@kuleuven.be

MASSIMILIANO PROIETTI holds a PhD from the Alta Scuola Europea di Scienze Religiose "Giuseppe Alberigo". His doctoral thesis dealt with the liturgical reform of Vatican II and its early implementation. He currently carries out his research activities at the John XXIII Foundation for Religious Studies in Bologna, and at the University of Modena and Reggio-Emilia. He contributes to the international research group coordinated by FSCIRE on the Creed of Nicaea and Constantinople.
   Address: Fondazione per le scienze religiose, Via San Vitale 114, 40125 Bologna, Italy
   Email: proietti@fscire.it

SAMUELE ADORNO graduated in classical philology from the University of Bologna, and is now a doctoral student at the John XXIII Foundation for Religious Sciences in Bologna. He is undertaking research on the history of the document "Theological Pluralism" published by the International Theological Commission in 1972.
   Address: Fondazione per le scienze religiose, Via San Vitale 114, 40125, Bologna, Italy
   Email: samuele.adorno@gmail.com

VALENTINA CICILIOT is an Associate Professor of contemporary Christianity, based at the Università Ca' Foscari in Venice. With a PhD. from the University of Reading and a Master's from Padua and Ca' Foscari, in 2016 she was awarded the Marie Skłodowska-Curie Fellowship to support her work on the origins of the Catholic charismatic movement. At the University of Notre Dame, South Bend, she studied the movement's inception in the US during the 1960s-1980s, illuminating its ties to European Catholicism and the role of women. Her publications include work on the history of the Catholic Renewal, female Catholicism and its transnational developments, American Catholicism and Evangelicalism, and canonization in the Catholic Church.

Address: Department of Humanities (DSU) Malcanton Marcorà Dorsoduro 3484/D, Calle Contarini 30123 Venezia, Italy.

Email: vciciliot@unive.it

SILVIA MARTÍNEZ CANO is graduate in Dogmatic Fundamental Theology. She has a doctorate in education, and a Master's in Visual Arts and Education. She is also a multidisciplinary artist - www.silviamartinezcano.es. Her areas of specialisation are interdisciplinary: The Ministry of God, Anthropology, Theology, Aesthetical Theology, Theory of Education, Art and Aesthetics, Social Pedagogy, and General Studies of Gender and Intersectionality. Currently she is a professor at the Faculty of Education of UCM and the San Pío X Institute of the Universidad Pontificia de Salamanca.

Address: Universidad Complutense de Madrid, Facultad de Educación – Centro de Formación del Profesorado, Edificio La Almudena C/ Rector Royo Villanova, 1 Ciudad Universitaria 28040 - Madrid, España

Email: silmar17@ucm.es

LUCA FERRACCI is Assistant Professor at the University of Modena and Reggio Emilia, and Research Fellow at the John XXIII Foundation for Religious Studies in Bologna. He is the editor of the Brill series A History of the Desire for Christian Unity and member of the editorial board of Concilium.

Address: Fondazione per le scienze religiose, Via San Vitale 114, 40125 Bologna, Italy

Email: lferracc@unimore.it

JOHANNES OELDEMANN PhD is a Catholic theologian and Director of the Johann Adam Moehler Institute for Ecumenism in Paderborn (Germany). He is primarily involved in Orthodox-Catholic dialogue and heads the German Bishops' Conference's scholarship program for Orthodox theologians. He was appointed by the Vatican as a member of the Faith and Order Commission for the 2023-30 term of office.

Address: Johann-Adam-Möhler-Institut für Ökumenik, Leostr. 19 a, 33098 Paderborn, Deutschland

Email: j.oeldemann@moehlerinstitut.de

FÁINCHE RYAN is Associate Professor of Systematic Theology, Trinity College Dublin, and Vice-President of the European Society of Catholic Theology. Recent publications include "The University: A Refuge of Truth and Truthfulness" in Theology and the University, (Routledge, 2024). Research focus: truth and truth-telling, the formation of sensus fidei, Thomas Aquinas.

Address: Loyola Institute, School of Religion, Theology, and Peace Studies, Trinity College Dublin, the University of Dublin, College Green Dublin 2. D02 PN40 Ireland

Email: faryan@tcd.ie

STEVEN BATTIN is author of Intercommunal Ecclesiology: The Church, Salvation, and Intergroup Conflict. He is an Assistant Professor at the University of Notre Dame.

Address: University of Notre Dame, 140 Malloy, Notre Dame, IN 46556

Email: sbattin.nd@gmail.com

Translators

FRANCIS MCDONAGH read classics at Cambridge and learned German on the side. He then worked in religious publishing for a number of years in Britain and Germany. He has spent the rest of his career in international development, including some years in Brazil with Oxfam and later based in London with the Catholic development agency CAFOD working on the Andean region. He writes for the Catholic

Contributors

weekly *The Tablet* on Latin America.
   Email: fmcdinho@yahoo.com

MAX SERJEANT is a writer and translator. He has a masters degree in Latin American Studies from the University of Leiden and an undergraduate degree in anthroloplogy from Brunel University. His research interests include the role of clergy in Central American social movements and cooperative models of economic development. He is the founder of the Latin American History podcast and has written for the Latin American News Dispatch, Anglican publisher Hymns Ancient and Modern and costarica.org among others.
   Email: maxserjeant@gmail.com

Vision & Mission

What *Concilium* is
Concilium is a journal of Catholic and Ecumenical theological reflection. Founded in the wake of the Second Vatican Council, it seeks to reinterpret and re-apply its vision of openness to new cultural contexts, and to changing social and religious realities. Led by the Spirit, the journal embraces multiple expressions of faith and spirituality arising from cultural plurality as a mark of its catholicity.

The aim of the journal
The aim of *Concilium* is to contribute to the transformation of the world and the Church in light of the Gospel. The journal is particularly committed to challenging structures of oppression and discrimination, and to doing theology from the perspective of the victims of social, economic and ecological inequality. It thus supports a new ecclesial imagination beyond patriarchy, clericalism, racism, anthropocentrism, monocultural hegemony, and the exploitation of the earth's resources.

The way we do theology
The mission of *Concilium* is reflected in the conciliar way of doing theology that we adopt as a community of theologians from various contexts. Inspired by the vision of the journal's founders, we provide a meeting place for a global conversation inviting diverse perspectives on important theological issues. Theologizing from the perspective of the margins and of ecological care are central commitments of *Concilium*. Thus, the journal *Concilium* and its conferences seek to draw attention to the voices and the theological questions and concerns of local and regional communities in a spirit of listening. Our meetings and structures aim to represent collegiality, shared leadership, mutuality, and transparency of decision making. As editors, we are committed to fair and sustainable relationships among ourselves and with our publishers, readers and authors.

Academic standards and digital presence
Concilium's journal issues strive to maintain academic standards. We remain connected to and draw deeply from the experiences and wisdom of marginalized communities. In order to further our mission, we seek to expand beyond traditional print media and develop a robust digital presence to improve access and participation.

CONCILIUM
International Journal of Theology

FOUNDERS
Anton van den Boogaard; Paul Brand; Yves Congar OP; Hans Küng; Johann-Baptist Metz; Karl Rahner SJ; Edward Schillebeeckx OP

BOARD OF DIRECTORS
President: Susan Abraham
Vice-Presidents: Luca Ferracci, Margareta Gruber, Leonel Guardado, Stan Chu Ilo

BOARD OF EDITORS
Susan Abraham, Berkeley (USA)
Antony John Baptist, Bangalore (India)
Steven Battin, Indiana (USA)
Bernardeth Caero Bustillos, Cochabamba (Bolivia)
Silvia Martínez-Cano, Madrid (Spain)
Viorel Coman, Bucharest (Romania)
Catherine Cornille, Boston (USA)
Geraldo Luiz De Mori SJ, Belo Horizonte (Brazil)
Massimo Faggioli, Villanova (USA)
Luca Ferracci, Bologna (Italy)
Margareta Gruber OSF, Vallendar (Germany)
Leonel Guardado, New York (USA)
Jonas Hagedorn, Bochum (Germany)
Stan Chu Ilo, Chicago (USA)
Léonard Amossou Katchekpele, Frankenthal (Germany)
Cesar Kuzma, Curitiba (Brazil)
Ludovic Lado SJ, N'Djamena (Chad)
Albertus Bagus Laksana, Yogyakarta (Indonesia)
Carlos Schickendantz, Santiago (Chile)
Stephan van Erp OP, Leuven (Belgium)
Wai Ching Angela Wong, Sha Tin (Hong Kong)
Richard L. Wood, Los Angeles/ Albuquerque (USA)
Antonina Wozna, Valencia (Spain)

PUBLISHERS
Hymns Ancient & Modern (London, United Kingdom) https://concilium.hymnsam.co.uk/
Verlag Karl Alber (Nomos) (Baden-Baden, Germany) https://concilium.nomos.de
Editrice Queriniana (Brescia, Italy) https://www.queriniana.it/concilium
Editorial Verbo Divino (Estella, Spain) http://www.revistaconcilium.com

Concilium General Secretariat:
Couvent de l'Annonciation
222 rue du Faubourg Saint-Honoré
75008 – Paris (France)
secretariat.concilium@gmail.com
Executive secretary: Kim S. Mendoza

Website: https://concilium-vatican2.org **Social Media:** https://linktr.ee/ConciliumINT

CONCILIUM FORMER EDITORS

Alberto Melloni (Italy)
Alois Müller (Switzerland)
Aloysius Pieris, S.J. (Sri Lanka)
† Alphonse Ngindu Mushete (Democratic Republic of Congo)
† André Hellegers (United States of America)
† Andrew Greeley (United States of America)
† Anne Carr (United States of America)
† Anton Weiler (Netherlands)
† August Wilhelm von Eiff (Germany)
† Barbara Ward Jackson (United States of America)
† Bas van Iersel, S.M.M. (Netherlands)
Ben van Baal (Netherlands)
† Bruce Vawter (United States of America)
† Carlo Colombo (Italy)
† Casiano Floristán (Spain)
† Charles Davis (England)
† Christian Duquoc, O.P. (France)
Christoph Theobald S.J. (France)
Christophe Boureux, O.P. (France)
† Christos Yannarás (Greece)
† Claude Geffré O.P. (France)
Daniel Marguerat (Switzerland)
† David Power, O.M.I. (Italy)
David Tracy (United States of America)
Dennis Gira (France)
Dietmar Mieth (Switzerland)
E. Hammerstein (Netherlands)
Eamonn Conway (Ireland)
† Elaine Wainwright (New Zealand)
Elisabeth Schüssler Fiorenza (United States of America)
Ellen van Wolde (Netherlands)
† Éloi Messi Metogo (Cameroon)
Elsa Tamez (Costa Rica)
François Kabasele Lumbala (Democratic Republic of Congo)
† Franz Böckle (Germany)
† Giuseppe Alberigo (Italy)
Giuseppe Ruggieri (Italy)
† Godfrey Diekmann, O.S.B. (United States of America)
† Gregory Baum, O.S.A. (Canada)
Gustavo Gutiérrez (Peru)
Hans Karl-Josef Kuschel (Germany)
† Harald Weinrich (Germany)
† Henri de Lubac, S.J. (France)
† Herman Schmidt, S.J. (Italy)
Hermann Häring (Germany)
† Jacques-Marie Pohier, O.P. (France)
† James Provost (United States of America)
Jan Peters, S.J. (Netherlands)
Janet Martin Soskice (United Kingdom)
† Jean Ladrière (Belgium)
† Jean Rémy (Belgium)
† Jean-Pierre Jossua, O.P. (France)
† Johannes Wagner (Germany)
† John Coleman, S.J. (United States of America)
John Panagopoulos (Greece)
John Zizoulas (United Kingdom)
† Jorge Mejía (Argentina)
† José Luis Aranguren (Spain/ United States of America)
José Oscar Beozzo (Brazil)
† Juan Alfaro, S.J. (Italy)
† Julia Ching (Canada)
† Jürgen Moltmann (Germany)
† Karl Lehmann (Germany)
Karl-Josef Kuschel (Germany)
† Knut Walf (Netherlands)
† Leo Alting von Geusau (Netherlands)
Leonardo Boff (Brazil)
Linda Hogan (Ireland)
Louis-Marie Chauvet (France)
† Luciano Caglioti (Italy)
† Ludolph Baas (Netherlands)
† Luigi Sartori (Italy)

† Luis Maldonado (Spain)
M. Palazzi (Netherlands)
Mary Shawn Copeland (United States of America)
Marciano Vidal, C.S.s.R. (Spain)
Maria Pilar Aquino Vargas (United States of America)
† Mariasusai Dhavamony S.J. (Italy)
† Marie-Dominique Chenu, O.P. (France)
Marie-Theres Wacker (Germany)
† Mary Collins, O.S.B. (United States of America)
Mary John Mananzan, O.S.B. (Philippines)
† Mateus Cardoso Peres, O.P. (Portugal)
Maureen Junker-Kenny (Ireland)
Mercy Amba Oduyoye (Ghana)
† Miklós Tomka (Hungary)
† Neophytos Edelby (Syria)
† Nicholas Lash (United Kingdom)
† Norbert Greinacher (Germany)
Norbert Mette (Germany)
Paul D. Murray (United Kingdom)
† Paul Ricoeur (France)
Paul Schotsmans (Belgium)
Paul Vos (Netherlands)
† Paulo Freire (Switzerland)
† Pedro Lain Entralgo (Spain)
† Peter Huizing, S.J. (Netherlands)
† Pierre Benoit, O.P. (Jordan)
† René Laurentin (France)
† Roberto Tucci (Italy)
† Roger Aubert (Belgium)
† Roland Murphy, O.Carm. (United States of America)
† Seán Freyne (Ireland)
† Teodoro Jiménez Urresti (Spain)
Teresa Okure, S.H.C.J. (Nigeria)
† Virgil Elizondo (United States of America)
Walter Kasper (Germany)
Werner Jeanrond (Ireland)

† Willem Beuken, S.J. (Netherlands)
William Bassett (United States of America)
Agbonkhianmeghe Orobator, S.J. (Kenya)
Andrés Torres Queiruga (Spain)
Anne-Béatrice Faye, C.I.C. (Senegal)
Carlos Mendoza-Álvarez, O.P. (Mexico/United States of America)
Daniel Franklin Pilario, C.M. (Philippines)
Diego Irarrázaval (Chile)
Enrico Galavotti (Italy)
Erik Borgman (Netherlands)
Esther Mombo (Kenya)
Felix Wilfred (India)
Gusztáv Kovács (Hungary)
Hille Haker (United States of America)
Huang Po-Ho (Taiwan)
João J. Vila-Chã, S.J. (Italy)
Jon Sobrino, S.J. (El Salvador)
Léonard Santedi Kinkupi (Democratic Republic of Congo)
Lisa Sowle Cahill (United States of America)
Luiz Carlos Susin, O.F.M. Cap. (Brazil)
Maria Clara Bingemer (Brazil)
Marie-Theres Wacker (Germany)
Michel Andraos (United States of America)
Michelle Becka (Germany)
Mile Babić, O.F.M. (Bosnia-Herzegovina)
Regina Ammicht Quinn (Germany)
Sarojini Nadar (South Africa)
Sharon A. Bong (Malaysia)
Silvia Scatena (Italy)
Solange Lefebvre (Canada)
Stefanie Knauss (United States of America)
Susan A. Ross (United States of America)
Thierry-Marie Courau, O.P. (France)
Gianluca Montaldi FN, (Italy)

The Canterbury Dictionary of
HYMNOLOGY

The result of over ten years of research by an international team of editors, The Canterbury Dictionary of Hymnology is the major online reference work on hymns, hymn-writers and traditions.

www.hymnology.co.uk

CHURCH TIMES

The Church Times, founded in 1863, has become the world's leading Anglican newspaper. It offers professional reporting of UK and international church news, in-depth features on faith, arts and culture, wide-ranging comment and all the latest clergy jobs. Available in print and online.

www.churchtimes.co.uk

Crucible

Crucible is the Christian journal of social ethics. It is produced quarterly, pulling together some of the best practitioners, thinkers, and theologians in the field. Each issue reflects theologically on a key theme of political, social, cultural, or environmental significance.

www.cruciblejournal.co.uk

JLS

Joint Liturgical Studies offers a valuable contribution to the study of liturgy. Each issue considers a particular aspect of liturgical development, such as the origins of the Roman rite, Anglican Orders, welcoming the Baptised, and Anglican Missals.

www.jointliturgicalstudies.co.uk

magnet

Magnet is a resource magazine published three times a year. Packed with ideas for worship, inspiring artwork and stories of faith and justice from around the world.

www.ourmagnet.co.uk

An invaluable resource for the contemporary preacher, each issue contains features on developing your preaching, in-depth reflections and lectionary sermons for the 13 Sundays following publication.

www.collegeofpreachers.co.uk

First published in 1965, Concilium has long been known for cutting-edge, critical and constructive theological thinking. The journal features the work of theologians from five continents.

www.concilium.hymnsam.co.uk

For more information on these publications visit the websites listed above or contact Hymns Ancient & Modern: Tel.: +44 (0)1603 785 910 Write to: Subscriptions, Hymns Ancient & Modern, 13a Hellesdon Park Road, Norwich NR6 5DR

Founders' Memorial Issue

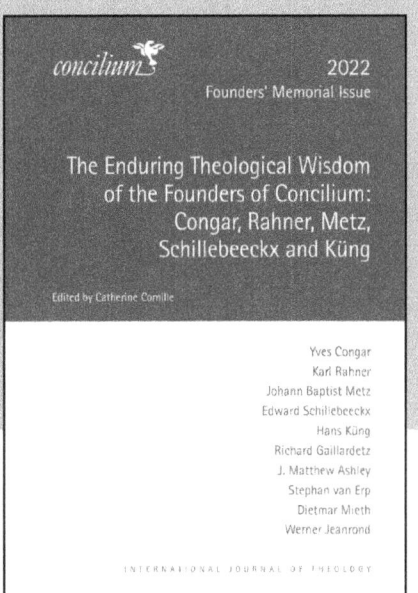

In April of 2021, the last of the founders of Concilium passed away. With the passing of this original generation, we thought it appropriate to pay tribute to the founders by republishing some of their seminal articles.

In this special memorial issue, read **Yves Congar** on the Church; **Karl Rahner** on Christianity and ideology; **Edward Schillebeeckx** on the Magisterium; **Johann Baptist Metz** on theodicy; and **Hans Küng** on a world ethic.

The original articles are accompanied by commentary from **Richard Gaillardetz**, **J. Matthew Ashley**, **Stephan van Erp**, **Dietmar Mieth** and **Werner Jeanrond**.

The Founders' Memorial Issue is available to read free on the Concilium website:

concilium.hymnsam.co.uk

Concilium Subscription Information

February   **2025/1:** *Nicaea*

April   **2025/2:** *Sacramentality*

July   **2025/3:** *Prison*

October   **2025/4**: *Comparative Theology*

December   **2025/5:** *Pain and Solace*

New subscribers: to receive the next five issues of Concilium please copy this form, complete it in block capitals and send it with your payment to the address below. Alternatively subscribe online at www.conciliumjournal.co.uk

Please enter my annual subscription for Concilium starting with issue 2025/2.

Individuals
____ £52 UK
____ £75 overseas and (Euro €92, US $110)

Institutions
____ £75 UK
____ £95 overseas and (Euro €120, US $145)

Postage included – airmail for overseas subscribers

Payment Details:
Payment can be made by cheque or credit card.
a. I enclose a cheque for £/$/€ ____ Payable to Hymns Ancient and Modern Ltd
b. To pay by Visa/Mastercard please contact us on +44(0)1603 785911 or go to www.conciliumjournal.co.uk

Contact Details:
Name ....
Address ....
....
Telephone .... E-mail ....

Send your order to *Concilium,* **Hymns Ancient and Modern Ltd**
13a Hellesdon Park Road, Norwich NR6 5DR, UK
E-mail: concilium@hymnsam.co.uk
or order online at www.conciliumjournal.co.uk

Customer service information
All orders must be prepaid. Your subscription will begin with the next issue of Concilium. If you have any queries or require Information about other payment methods, please contact our Customer Services department.

www.ingramcontent.com/pod-product-compliance
Lightning Source LLC
Chambersburg PA
CBHW062038290426
44109CB00026B/2659